D0028674

LET THE
CHILDREN
COME

A New
Approach to
Children's Sermons

BRANT D. BAKER

Augsburg ▪ Minneapolis

LET THE CHILDREN COME
A New Approach to Children's Sermons

Copyright © 1991 Augsburg Fortress. All rights reserved. Except for brief quotations in critical articles or reviews, no part of this book may be reproduced in any manner without prior written permission from the publisher. Write to: Permissions, Augsburg Fortress, 426 S. Fifth St., Box 1209, Minneapolis, MN 55440.

Scripture quotations unless otherwise noted are from the New Revised Standard Version Bible, copyright © 1989, Division of Christian Education of the National Council of the Churches of Christ in the United States of America.

Scripture quotations marked RSV are from the Revised Standard Version of the Bible, copyright © 1946, 1952, and 1971 by the Division of Christian Education of the National Council of Churches.

Excerpt from *Christian Religious Education* by Thomas A. Groome, copyright © 1980 Thomas A. Groome. Reprinted by permission of HarperCollins, Publishers, Inc.

Cover design: Lecy Design
Internal design: Judy Gilats, Peregrine Publications

Library of Congress Cataloging-in-Publication Data

Baker, Brant D., 1958–
    Let the children come : a new approach to children's sermons / Brant D. Baker.
        p.   cm.
    Includes bibliographical references and index.
    ISBN 0-8066-2545-7
    1. Preaching to children.   2. Children's sermons.   I. Title.
BV4235.C4B34   1991
252'.53—dc20   91-8876
                                                                            CIP

The paper used in this publication meets the minimum requirements of American National Standard for Information Sciences—Permanence of Paper for Printed Library Materials, ANSI Z329.48-1984. ∞™

Manufactured in the U.S.A.   AF 9-2545

95   94   93   92   91   1   2   3   4   5   6   7   8   9   10

The speech of the community is also action, and if its whole speech and action are a praise of God, this praise . . . has its own specific place and form in the ministry of the community.

—Karl Barth, *Church Dogmatics*

To my parents,
who taught me how to love as a child,
to my wife, Karen,
who keeps the child in me alive.

CONTENTS

INTRODUCTION

Experiential Christianity

If you could do anything you wanted in a children's sermon, anything at all, what would you do? Let your mind roam free over the possibilities: a trip to Jerusalem to see the Mount of Olives, a conversation with the Apostle Paul to discuss the finer points of his letter to the Romans, a boat ride across the Sea of Galilee to feel the wind and the waves that Jesus once stilled. The possibilities seem endless for helping children understand Christianity by helping them *experience* Christianity.

And that is exactly the point.

There is no cause for glazed eyes and inattentive squirms except that too often those entrusted with delivering children's sermons put more emphasis on *sermon* than on *children*. A children's sermon has every opportunity to be dynamic, creative, and exciting.

Dynamic. Experiential Christianity suggests that we apply what we know about children to the art of the children's sermon. Children live not so much in the world of thought and reflection as in the world of experiences, relationships, and interactions. Children (not to mention the rest of us) learn best with methods that meet them where they are.

Creative. Experiential Christianity suggests that we attempt to recover the creative faculty and bring it to bear on children's sermons. We all possess the ability to be creative by virtue of being created in the image of God. Applying that creativity to the special circumstances of the children's sermon has enormous potential.

Exciting. Experiential Christianity suggests that we attempt to stimulate children through children's sermons by stimulating the congregation as well. We could say that part of everyone who sits in the congregation is nothing more than a grown-up child. That part of us isn't content to just sit and watch: we want to play, too. Children's sermons offer the consummate intergenerational teaching experience.

There is a structure of teaching methods that all teachers have experienced and to which most teachers subscribe. It runs something as follows:

Learn by hearing.
Learn by watching.
Learn by doing.

Thankfully, the last decade has witnessed a shift in the nature of the church's teaching methods from an emphasis on hearing to an emphasis on doing. An example of this shift to participatory education is the movement from lecture-oriented class time to discussion-oriented class time in which students learn as they are involved in a process through questions and answers, dialogue and debate.

Put simply, the basic premise of experiential Christianity is to ask, "Why just talk about a disciple when we can become one? Why just say something that can be sung? Why just speak of a place when we can create it in our midst and go there? Why just tell the story when we can act it out?"

In the church year we look to create moments of experiential Christianity at outstanding points along the way, holidays such as Christmas and Easter, special worship services, congregational retreats, and youth work camps. Occasionally a special need in the church family or community will provide opportunity for people to roll up their sleeves and encounter God and themselves as they encounter human need. The sacraments, instituted through our Lord's wisdom to involve us heart, soul, mind, and body in God's grace, provide the most outstanding opportunities for experiential Christianity. In God's glorious plan, almost all the activities of a faith community have their own particular purposes but can also end up becoming life-changing educational moments for those involved.

The challenge, however, is to create such encounters in the day-to-day or week-to-week educational life of the household of God. These are educational encounters wherein the truth of God surrounds and pervades, transcendent moments that leave us forever changed and hungry, glimpses of incarnational mystery and meaning. None of this ever happens but for the grace of God. Yet we too are players, again by grace. Our part is to prompt and to facilitate and to create time ripe for experiential encounters, time ripe with possibilities for knowing God.

The Biblical Basis
Are children's sermons up to this challenge? Do they serve a valid purpose in worship? Are they really worth the effort? Honest answers are important here because our view of the place of a children's sermon in worship not only defines how much time and effort we give to their development, but also goes a long way toward suggesting what we could try to do in the time given.

The motives for a separate moment in worship for children are mixed. For many people the purpose is an earnest desire to instruct children. Others use the time to instruct the adults. Still others simply want children to feel a part of worship.

In fact what the children's sermon provides is an opportunity for children to be loved by an adult in an intentional way, not through some incidental time in worship, but through an *incarnational reality* that creates love, understanding, and belonging. As God is incarnationally with us, so we are incarnationally with the children.

It is striking that most children's sermons could be given whether or not any children are present to hear them. This lamentable absence of relationship between presenter and child stands in stark contradiction to the model supplied by God:

The Word became flesh
and dwelt among us . . .

Incarnation, the word taking on human form and function, is a relational model for teaching. God did more than speak the Word to us, God became flesh that we might learn the truth in our own flesh. For the giver of children's sermons, an incarnational model means bringing more than words to the Word: it means bringing one's self, it means bringing thorough preparation, it means bringing activity, movement, and experience of the truth.

In short, living an incarnational reality means giving to these most important children of God the *best* of all that we have to offer.

Incarnation also means risking, because to "dwell among" means giving up the distance between child and adult, between preacher and participant. That risk may take the form of a hug, it may come forth in a grown man or woman wiggling or leaping, making a funny face or a funny sound, it may mean being stopped cold by a response from a child and losing our self-composure. But risking is fundamental to incarnation, and incarnation is fundamental to knowing truth. Thanks be to God that by grace we are strengthened in knowing that these risks serve the goal of the kingdom.

A thoughtful critique of a separate children's time has been made by David Ng and Virginia Thomas in their excellent book, *Children in the Worshiping Community*. Their concern is for the place of children in worship as a whole. They worry that the children's sermon is a poor solution to a larger problem, relegating the place of children in worship to one patronizing five-minute segment so that there is no longer call to think of them or their special needs. They continue,

> We may one day be convinced that such a practice has suffi-
> cient merit to justify its practice. For now we can see mostly
> problems associated with children's sermons. For one, there is
> the problem of overemphasis on participation at an intellectual
> and cognitive level, skewing the balance away from the emo-
> tive and affective levels. Especially for younger children, this
> is inappropriate and may leave a residue impression about faith
> as solely an intellectual pursuit. The truth is that very few chil-
> dren's sermons reflect much intellectual and theological integri-
> ty. Rather, they tend toward moralisms which reinforce a notion
> that the gospel means to be able to do the right thing in order
> to gain God's rewards.[1]

Not surprisingly, children's sermons that overemphasize the intellectual and cognitive level tend toward moralisms, but it is just this that an incarnational model of doing children's sermons seeks to avoid. To have theological integrity, a gospel communication must meet us at all levels of our being, and may need to leave us without a tidy answer—even for children. What can be left with them is an experience that holds a truth deeper than words.

The Developmental Basis

The origin of the children's sermon or storytime was perhaps just that, a story. Storytelling is, on the whole, a marvelous tool for bringing about experiential Christianity. The value of a story is that it allows the listener to participate vicariously with the characters, actually *experiencing* the events, decisions, and emotions that confront them. The difficulty is that storytelling is by and large a lost art. To simply recite the facts of the story is not enough—emotion, imagery, and expression must all be present as "handles" by which the listener grabs hold of the story.

It is easy to suppose that as time went on, and scores of uninitiated children's storytellers struggled, learning by hearing was augmented or replaced by the fabled object lesson—learning by watching. A brown paper bag became the necessary extension of any children's sermon. The problem with most (not all) object lessons, however, is that they fail to take seriously the work of those who tell us how children think and learn. The most notable of these, Jean Piaget, has suggested that the ability for abstract thought does not emerge until relatively late in childhood development, somewhere around the ages of twelve to fourteen (Stage 3).[2] The children who come forward for children's sermons are probably somewhat younger than this, varying from two to twelve, depending on the tradition of the church. Their thinking is in what Piaget called Stage 1 or 2, a more concrete type of thinking that carries with it no ability for reflection, that is, no ability to think about thinking and thus construct the theories that enable a person to evaluate, assume roles, or project change. This lack of ability for abstract thought undercuts most object lessons, which are based on making a comparison between the object and some religious truth. Thus to tell children in an object lesson that the resurrection of Jesus Christ is like a caterpillar becoming a butterfly may confuse more than clarify. The leap required between the object and its faith analogy is beyond their present ability.

The recognition of the developmental stages in a child's thought is a golden opportunity for children's sermons that are experiential. As Ng and Thomas observe, "A delightful bonus which comes with this type of thinking [Stage 1] is that the children are capable of an imagination which is unencumbered by logic. They are free to take an image, or a daydream, or a bit of reality, and through imagination soar any distance in any direction."[3] Putting this imaginative capacity to work is simply another form of experience, and its use enables us to pretend we are on a boat or in a crowd, that we are musical notes or braying goats, or that we are seeing the Jerusalem temple or the wall of an Egyptian city in what is, in fact, merely the pulpit.

The work of Erik Erikson regarding the psychosocial development in children sheds further light on the realities and the possibilities of children's sermons.[4] These ages encompass the tasks of initiative and industry in Erikson's theory. Key to initiative (roughly ages two to six) is the newfound locomotive ability of the child and a corresponding curiosity to explore an expanding world. In terms of children in church, this may well mean taking time to explore the cavernous expanse of space inside the sanctuary, while at the same time sanctioning vigorous movement in the exploration. Running, crawling, skipping, and wiggling not only epitomize learning by doing but help overcome stereotypes of church as a stiff and somber place. There must be respect in worship, but there should also be joy! The task of industry (ages six to puberty) is to produce things, to work together to make something. In terms of the children's sermon this may mean being co-creators, working together to make the sermon itself happen by being the characters in a skit, giving verbal responses, or perhaps learning a new skill like the sign language version of the Lord's Prayer. This working together to create and to learn fits well with the goals of experiential Christianity.

The Educational Basis

In his book, *Christian Religious Education: Sharing Our Story and Vision*, Thomas Groome outlines five movements to an educational approach he calls "shared praxis" (practice).[5] The background and full explanation of this approach are worth exploring. Groome suggests that there are five movements in the study of any given topic:

   1. The participants are invited to name their own activity concerning the topic for attention.
   2. They are invited to reflect on why they do what they do, and what the likely or intended consequences of their actions are.
   3. The educator makes present to the group the Christian community's story concerning the topic at hand and the faith response it invites.

4. The participants are invited to appropriate God's story to their lives in a dialectic with their own stories.
5. There is an opportunity to choose a personal faith response for the future.[6]

Groome allows for flexibility and fluidity among the five movements in practice, meaning in part that they need not necessarily occur in this order or all in the same segment of time. The main vehicle for the first two movements is questioning (which is a good form of participatory education). The third movement is the place where "teaching" as it is traditionally thought of takes place. Groome's thesis is that limiting teaching to a one-sided flow of information (i.e., defining teaching as the third movement only) makes for shallow learning. Hence he fills out the educational process with questioning at the first and second movements, a dialogical approach to the third movement and the follow-through of the last two movements.

That follow-through is most intentionally helped by the teacher in the fourth movement, during which the students are asked to look for the meeting of God's story with their own story. The fifth movement is a second meeting, this time of God's vision with their own vision.

Given the time constraints in the typical children's sermon, this fifth movement must often be left to the spirit. Comfort can be had in knowing that much of our learning is done after the teaching in any educational model. One way to help the fifth movement encounter may come along the lines of suggested "things to do this week." For the most part, however, we plant the seed and trust God for the harvest.

In the context of the children's sermon, it is a synthesis of the third and fourth movements that produces learning by doing, or experiential Christianity. An example of this is a children's sermon on the role of the congregational promises made on behalf of the child in baptism or dedication as described on page 85, "A Church Full of Parents." It might begin with first and second movement questions such as "How many parents do you have?" and "What do they do for you?" The kinds of things that parents do might be summarized by identifying examples—parents provide for them, guide and discipline them, and teach them. Next the third movement and fourth movement (presentation and experience) are set up by reference to the promises the congregation makes at each child's baptism or dedication to act like a parent. "So, will everyone who is not a parent of one of the children up front please stand . . . and let me introduce you (taking a child by the hand) to your 'new' church parent" (leaving the child with someone and going back for another). While the experience (fourth movement) of this particular truth is going on, the presentation (third movement) continues. Parallels are made along the lines of the earlier examples as to what *church* parents do: provide resources, guidance, and Christian education.

Perhaps the best description of learning by doing is given by Walter Wink. In a discussion of left brain and right brain theory, Wink emphasizes the need to call on both hemispheres of the brain if people are to be truly "transformed" as they learn. A lesson learned in this way can "cause the insights it fosters to be experienced as a 'felt sense' within the body. If this feeling is lived with until it becomes objectified in art or act or articulated in words, the truth that the text bears has come a long way toward incarnation in our very flesh."[7] To paraphrase: the gospel message must be actually experienced physically, and then expressed, in order for us to begin our own incarnation of its truth. To incarnate the gospel is the goal of experiential Christianity; to involve the total person in the hearing and subsequent pronouncement of the gospel of Jesus Christ is the desired result.

About the Creative Process
To be created in the image of God means, at the very least, that we are created to be creators. To create is to experience not only the joy of showing forth a mixture of self and world in a new way, but it is even more to take part in the very work and nature of the Creator.

One of the most crucial challenges of educational ministry is creativity. The children's sermons in the pages that follow are offered as examples of the incarnational and experiential model outlined above. Creating new sermons in this model will come from understanding its theological and theoretical basis and from understanding how to focus the creative process. That process, in giving birth to these children's sermons, ran roughly as follows:

1. Definition of the general topic, text, theme, idea, to be communicated, usually at least two days in advance.
2. Dreaming the question: "If we could do anything to experience this topic or text, *anything*, what would we do?"

3. Assessment of resources on hand: people, objects, and places usually being the main resources to draw on.
4. Modification of the dream to reality.

The keys to this process are the *time frame* and the *absolute seriousness* of dreaming the question. Trying to develop an experiential children's sermon on Saturday afternoon denies the time frame needed to take dreaming the question seriously, let alone the time necessary to make the needed arrangements. Probably not a few presenters come up with the great ideas for children's sermons, but reckon that there is too little time left to implement them. Using this process lets us enjoy the full fruit of our creativity.

Usually the end result is not too far modified from the dream. A good example is Easter Sunday, the dream of which ran something like this: "Talk about resurrection is too abstract for the children. What if we could actually experience the thrill of the empty tomb?" This process of dreaming began several weeks before Easter, and from it came the idea of an encounter with Mary, structured in such a way as to take us from the sadness of the crucifixion to the joy of the resurrection. The rest of the drama followed once this central piece was in place (see "Mary's Story," page 49).

For most of my life I did not consider myself a creative person because I couldn't draw or sculpt. How much was missed! A narrow definition of creativity is by far the greatest hindrance to knowing the creative aspect of the image of God inside of us. Whatever creative process you use, become *aware* of your own creativity!

What to Do When
The children's sermons that follow have all been used with children. This means at the very least that they have been tried and proven. It also means that the reader benefits from seeing the unexpected responses children sometimes give. This is part of the risk of incarnation discussed above, but it can also be part of the joy. The main keys for handling such situations are 1) knowing where you are headed and 2) having a sense of humor.

Having a clear outline of the main points firmly in mind can keep wild or even embarrassing comments from getting things off track. No matter how well worded a question is, children often don't see where you thought you wanted to go. It is *always* appropriate to rephrase a question or even to answer the question yourself if need be. Knowing where you are headed means knowing which questions are worth struggling over and which are simply points along the way. In this regard timing is a part of knowing the outline: working too long and hard on a minor point is to miss the point; not giving the children long enough to come up with a major point is also to miss the point. Know which points are important, know generally how to get to them, and celebrate whatever detours come along the way.

The ability to laugh, with the children and at oneself, will go a long way in defusing some of the more outrageous things that inevitably *will* happen. One of my favorite such instances came in the sermon entitled "Gone Fishin'," pages 30–31. The point I wanted to make was that the miracle of the great catch of fish helped convince the disciples to follow Jesus. We had been pretending to be the disciples wrestling with that tremendous catch. One little fellow got so excited he held up a "fish" and said,

"I got a fish!"

"You got a *big* fish!" I exclaimed, then continued, *"Whew!* Now you're really tired. Well . . . what do you think those men did next after they caught all those fish?"

"Ate 'em," the little fisherman replied.

It is good to keep in mind that insofar as the congregation is not really so much an audience as participants, theirs is a sharing in the sermon in all its heavenly and earthly splendor. (Also, insofar as many of them are parents, they know about children's propensity to say embarrassing things.) It is good to keep in mind that the children won't be embarrassed by the remarks of their peers (although they may tend to make fun of them, to which a firm adult response is called for). Finally, it is good to keep in mind that we are all God's children in God's house doing God's business, and there is great joy and freedom in this.

About Using This Book

People involved in communication of the gospel know, or at least intuit, that the Word of God is inherently incarnational in nature. This is to say several things: It is to say that the same notes for any given children's sermon will come out differently each time it is done. It is to say that attempts to transplant these proclamations verbatim will not only come across as stiff but will also deny the spontaneity, creativity, and just plain fun that lurks in any communication event. It is to say that what is found in the following pages should be seen as outlines to be enfleshed by you and the children in your congregation.

One thing that will prevent wholesale transplant of these ideas is the difference of physical plant resources. As will be seen, "church geography" plays an important role in several of these events. The church you serve may have two aisles instead of one, a crowded chancel area that disallows too many folks on it at once, an oddly placed communion table, and so forth. Use what you've got! If you have two outside aisles and a smaller church, what a great place to march around Jericho seven times! If you have a balcony, why not go up there for a series of sermons on mountain tops (Noah, Abraham, Moses, Jesus, New Jerusalem)? In many ways the geography of the church building is a "text" waiting for interpretation: the potential you find in it will depend on how carefully and how creatively you study it.

A brief word on the congregation. Unless you are blessed with an extremely flexible group, it may take a few months of using these kinds of children's sermons before the congregation realizes that they are allowed, and in some cases expected, to participate. But once the people do understand that they too are going to enjoy the surprise of the gospel, they may become more pliable and quick to respond.

It might be a good idea to start by using the sermons that you perceive to be less "threatening" to your congregation. By the time I came up with the idea for "Parting the Red Sea" (page 20), the congregation was so used to my strange requests that they jumped up and moved without hesitation. Building the trust for making unusual requests and learning how to communicate unusual ideas to large groups of people both take time.

A brief word on numbers. Many of the sermons that follow would work far better with smaller groups than those with which they were originally done (20–30). It is the rare case that smaller groups are not preferable; again, this is one of the resources to be considered as you create experiential learning events.

Finally, it has taken several years to come up with enough children's sermons that truly fit the methodology of experiential Christianity to fill a book. The task is a hard and challenging one but not without the rewards that creativity brings. It is to be hoped that the ideas here will be sparks to your own creations of experiential Christianity, as God's Spirit of creativity begins to move us in a new direction.

God bless.

BIBLE STORIES

PARTING THE RED SEA

Scripture: Exodus 14:21-31
Focus: There is a lot to be afraid of in this world, for children and adults alike. Whether we are being chased by Pharaoh's army or the fears of modern life, God calls us to trust.
Experience: To be present at the parting of the Red Sea by having the children become the children of Israel, having the ushers become Pharaoh's army, and having the congregation become the waters of the Red Sea.
Arrangements: Have at least four ushers or other adults on hand who know their cue and are ready to give chase to the children of Israel. If these sermons are new territory for the congregation, a printed word of instruction in the bulletin might help things come together more quickly.

LEADER: Would the children meet me at the back of the sanctuary please? Today we're going to pretend that we're the children of Israel, the Hebrew nation, escaping from the Egyptians. Do you remember that story? How Moses led the people out into the wilderness to escape from Pharaoh; how they came up against the Red Sea and couldn't cross with Pharaoh's armies closing in behind them? Well, we're going to do all that, so first of all we need somebody to be Moses. (*Choose a child.*) Good, you're Moses, and you come down here to the front of the children of Israel.

Congregation, we need your help. We need everybody to stand up and move into the aisle to become the Red Sea. Pretend that you're the ocean, if you want to do the wave that's fine . . .

OK, here's what happened (*read from Bible, Exodus 14:21*): "Then Moses stretched out his hand over the sea . . ."—OK, Moses, stretch out your hand . . . very good! "The Lord drove the sea back by a strong east wind all night, and turned the sea into dry land; and the waters were divided." (*Congregation should move back into pews, but make sure they don't sit down.*)

Great! Now the children of Israel went on through—congregation, don't sit down!—Moses, lead your nation on through here, all the children of Israel are walking through on dry land.

(*After arriving at the front of the church*) Where's Moses? Moses, it says here that when all of the people got through they looked back, and what did they see, but the Egyptians! (*Cue for ushers.*) Look at those menacing Egyptians! And it says that

Moses raised his hand—hurry Moses, raise your hand—and the ocean came back together. (*Congregation should catch their cue.*) Whew!

Well what does all this mean, why is it important? Moses, what does this tell us?

CHILD: I don't know.

L. Anybody have any ideas?

CHILDREN: To pray to God.

L: To pray to God, I think you're right. Because God is interested in us and wants to help us out, and is active in our lives, so we don't need to be afraid when we feel like there's no escape from our problems. Like Moses we can lift our hands in prayer and ask God to take over. Well, let's all lift our hands right now and ask God's help and thank God for the way we're taken care of. (*Prayer.*)

A WANDERING ARAMEAN

Scripture: Deuteronomy 26:5-11

Focus: Throughout the Old Testament God seems to have a special concern for the wanderer. Because Israel had herself once been a wanderer, God called on her to show special consideration for those foreign and often forlorn sojourners, whose journey was sometimes as much spiritual as physical.

Experience: To feel what it is like to be a wanderer by becoming a part of the Exodus. (This children's sermon was originally used on the eve of welcoming a refugee to the church.)

Arrangements: The congregation will enjoy this sermon more if your church is equipped with a radio microphone (you may want to run a check on its strength beforehand), but don't give up on it if one is not available to you—this is for the children, not the adults! Think through a route that will take you out of the church by one door and back in by another. The distance you cover will depend on how much time you usually take for the children's sermon and how big your group is. You will want to arrange for help holding all of the doors open on your route.

LEADER: Good morning! Good to see you all this morning! Let me ask you a question. What if we were sitting here and somebody said, "You've got to leave right now?" What would we do?

CHILDREN: We'd have to leave. . . ?

L: I guess we would. OK, let's go! Let's go this way . . . we have to leave. We are becoming refugees—we don't have a home. (*As you walk, review the story of Moses and the children of Israel. Due to the distraction of being mobile the children may need more prompting than normal to recall the story.*) Do you remember in the Bible anybody else who was a refugee, anybody else who didn't have a home and who had to leave? How about Moses? What did Moses do? He took the children of Israel out of Egypt and led them through the wilderness. They were in the wilderness, homeless, wandering, not sure where they were going. They found that they had to trust God for all things, things they used to take for granted like shelter and food and even water. They found that there were lots of distractions along the way— Aaron, get out from behind that bush—that might keep them from getting to their final destination. Finally, they got to the promised land, to the home God had promised to them (*reenter sanctuary*). Well, a little like Moses and the children of Israel, we wandered through the wilderness and have finally come back to our home in God. Are we all back? I think we only lost a few outside . . .

How did you feel being a refugee, wandering through the wilderness? It was probably kind of fun for us, but you know some people have to leave their home and have no place to go. Even so, God loves them, and in the book of Deuteronomy God asks us to love them too, because we were once homeless in a different way, spiritually homeless, but God loved us and brought us back home through Jesus Christ. Let's pray and thank God for watching over us, and for giving us a spiritual home in this church through Jesus Christ. (*Prayer.*)

WELCOMING THE STRANGER

Scripture: Deuteronomy 10:19
Focus: In the church, to speak of "the household of God" is to speak of the very special set of relationships that exist because we share a common faith. The fact of that household means that each of us has countless moms and dads, aunts and uncles, brothers, sisters,

and children. It also means that there are no strangers in our midst, at least for very long!

Experience: To introduce ourselves to new members of the church.

Arrangements: Choose a Sunday when new members are joining. Try to have the new members sit together in a convenient location. You may want to clue them in as to what will happen during the children's sermon.

LEADER: Hello! Let me ask a question. Have you ever been a new person in a new place, been someplace for the first time, like the first day of school or something? And all the people around you are talking and being friends and you just kind of feel alone because you don't know anybody?

CHILDREN: Yes.

L: It's kind of scary, isn't it? A long time ago God knew that being a new person in a new place was kind of scary so the Bible tells the story of how the children of Israel, after finally getting to their new home, were told by God that they had better always remember what it felt like to be a stranger and that they had better always make strangers feel welcome.

Well you know, church can be that way sometimes for new people who come to be with us. It's a big place, lots of people, and everybody knows one another and says, "Hey, how you doing?" and if you're a new person it can be kind of overwhelming. Today the Matherlys are going to join our church: do you think maybe they feel a little bit like strangers, maybe feel a little bit scared?

C: Yes.

L: I wondered if it might be good for us to introduce ourselves to the Matherlys so that they could have some special friends here. This is Mr. and Mrs. Matherly, and Sarah Beth, who is about your age, and her little brother, David, who we just baptized. And you know, one neat thing about David is that in six or seven years when you all are going into junior high you may end up helping to teach David in church school. You may want especially to say "Hi" to him because someday you may see him in a special way.

How about if we all go stand up and shake the Matherlys' hands, and if you want to tell them who you are just introduce yourself to them and get to know them. (*Children engulf the Matherly family for several minutes!*)

I'm sure the Matherlys appreciated that. Now they know at least twenty people in the church a little bit better. And wherever we see them around, let's be sure to say "Hey, remember me?" Let's all hold hands and have a prayer thanking God that we're never strangers in the church. (*Prayer.*)

THE BATTLE OF JERICHO

Scripture: Joshua 6:1-21

Focus: The Old Testament is full of wonderful stories that tell us about the power of God and the faithfulness of God's people, especially in the face of seemingly insurmountable odds.

Experience: To reinact the fall of Jericho by having the children be the children of Israel and having the congregation become the wall of the city.

Arrangements: Determine beforehand what configuration you will use for the "wall." If there are two side aisles in your church and few children, you may decide to actually do the marching (once or all seven times) suggested by the Joshua passage. If the sanctuary has only one center aisle or the number of children is large, you may elect to move the children to the center aisle and have them turn in a circle seven times as they stand in place.

Regardless of what you do with the children, you will need three or four people at the end of each pew (which may necessitate their getting up and moving), as well as all the people in the first and last occupied pews, to form the wall of the city of Jericho. By using several people at the end of each pew, plus two or three rows of people in the front and the back of the church, you will hopefully end up with a rectangular wall that is several people thick, inside of which are still seated a few people who can be the inhabitants of Jericho. The wall should look something like one of the sketches on page 25. You may want to consider a note in the bulletin to help the congregation move more quickly into their places.

```
XXXXXXXXX  C   XXXXXXXXX
XXXXXXXXX  C C XXXXXXXXX
XXX           C C          XXX
XXX        C C            XXX
XXX        C C            XXX
XXX  Pews  C C  Pews  XXX
XXX        C C            XXX
XXX        C C            XXX
XXX        C C            XXX
XXXXXXXXX  C   XXXXXXXXX
XXXXXXXXX  ↓   XXXXXXXXX
```

A church with a center aisle.

C = children
X = adults who stand to form the wall

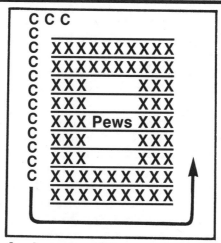

```
C C C
C
C   XXXXXXXXXX
C   XXXXXXXXXX
C   XXX      XXX
C   XXX      XXX
C   XXX Pews XXX
C   XXX      XXX
C   XXX      XXX
C   XXXXXXXXXX
    XXXXXXXXXX
```

A church with two aisles.

C = children
X = adults who stand to form the wall

LEADER: Come on down here close! (*As the children come forward instruct the congregation to stand as determined by where you want to place the "wall." Ask the appropriate pews and persons to move as necessary, explaining that they are to end up looking like a wall.*)

Do you all know the story about Joshua and the battle of Jericho? Well, this is the wall around Jericho, and we need to go out into the aisles, around the sides, along the front, and to pretend that we're the children of Israel surrounding the city. (*Or designate a child to be Joshua and begin leading the children around as you continue to tell the story.*) Good, we still need some children of Israel down this side over here . . . great! Well, it says in the Bible that the children of Israel marched around Jericho seven times, so let's turn around where we're standing seven times. (*If marching, say after a few times around, "Let's pretend that this is the seventh time.*) One, two, three, four . . . getting dizzy? . . . five, six, seven! And then the Bible says that the children of Israel gave a mighty shout, so let's give a mighty shout.

CHILDREN: Ahhhh!

L: And the walls fell down! (*Motion to congregation to sit; they should catch on well enough to know their cue.*) Well, some of the wall fell down faster than others . . . but that was good, that was good! OK, come on back to the front, children of Israel. Good job!

Did you have any doubt in your mind that the walls would come down when they were supposed to just now?

C: Yes. No.

L: A few had some doubts, others of us didn't. Well, I'm not certain I knew for sure myself. And that's a lot like what happened with Joshua and the children of Israel. They were small in number and strength compared to the people inside the city, they were scared, but they trusted enough to at least try and believe what God had told them, that the walls would come down. And so they marched, and they shouted, and the walls did come down. Children of Israel, let's have a prayer and thank God for the way God acts in mighty ways. (*Prayer.*)

BLOW ME DOWN!

Scripture: 1 Kings 18:17-40
Focus: The power of God is sometimes best seen when it is up against overwhelming odds. The power of God is also often understated. The focus of this sermon is the overwhelming, but quiet, power of God that is available even when we seem weak, powerless, and overwhelmed ourselves.
Experience: To pretend to be Elijah as he faces the 450 prophets of Baal and overcomes them with God's power. The congregation will serve as the prophets of Baal, and a simple breath of air will represent the power of God's Spirit.
Arrangements: None are needed, but if these kinds of sermons are still new to the congregation, you might consider placing a note in the bulletin asking that they stand when called upon, and then fall back into their seats when the "breath of God" blows over them.

LEADER: Great to see you all today! Have you ever felt like you were the only one who was trying to do the right thing, maybe at school on the playground, or playing with your friends in the backyard, that you were trying to be good while everyone else seemed to be bad?

CHILDREN: (*Some nods.*)

L: There's a story in the Bible about someone who felt that way, too. His name was Elijah, and he was God's prophet. One day Elijah challenged not just one, not just two, but 450 bad men! They were against God, and God asked Elijah to put them in their place. Would that be scary, 450 against one?

C: Yes.

L: What if you were the one, would you be scared?

C: Yes!

L: But what if God was on your side, would you still be scared?

C: Yes. No. Maybe.

L: Well, let's find out! Let's pretend we are Elijah, God's prophet. Why don't we stand up and move up onto the front of the church so we can see the congregation. And then we'll ask the congregation to stand up, because we're going to pretend that they're the 450 bad men that God asked Elijah to take care of. (*Congregation should stand, children should stand and face them, if possible from the chancel or the chancel steps.*)

Now, how do you think God helped Elijah put those 450 bad men in their place?

C: Don't know. Blew them up. Shot them.

L: You might think he would have to blow them up, there were so many, but what Elijah did was more like blow them down. Elijah knew that it would be God's power that would take care of them, not his own. What Elijah did was to call out to God and say, "Answer me, O Lord, answer me," and when God did it was almost like God's breath was enough to make those 450 bad men fall down! If we were to blow toward the congregation, like they were candles on a birthday cake, and they fell down, we might be able to feel a little bit what Elijah must have felt. Let's try that together, ready, one, two, three . . .

C: (*Blow.*)

L: (*While they are blowing*) Answer us, O Lord, answer us! (*A hand motion to the congregation might also help get them seated on cue.*)

Wow. What do you think of that? Just a few of us, and so many of them, but it worked! God is sure powerful, and now we know it the same way Elijah knew it. That was great!

Let's have a prayer and thank God that even when we feel like we're the only ones standing up for what is right, God's power is there to help us. (*Prayer.*)

FAITHFULNESS

Scripture: 1 Kings 18:41-46

Focus: Patience can be called a virtue. Religious patience can be called faithfulness. The focus of this sermon is to explore a link between the everyday virtue of patience and our calling as believers to be faithful.

Experience: To feel what Elijah's servant (and by extension, Elijah) must have felt when asked to look seven times for something that was not there.

Arrangements: Identify a place in the sanctuary to which you can send a child to look for something "unusual." The place should be close by and, if possible, behind a door or other structure that obscures the place from view of the children. Of course, nothing unusual will be found until you give the cue. You will need to ask an usher to place an object, such as a flower or a piece of candy, in the place the child has been looking after your verbal clue.

LEADER: Good morning everybody, how are you!? I need a volunteer. (*Choose a likely candidate.*) Would you go and look inside that door right over there, look to see if there is anything on the floor that looks unusual? Just go look and see what you find. (*As volunteer returns*) Anything on the floor?

CHILD: No.

L: No? Nothing? Imagine that. Well, listen, would you go look again, as long as you're up . . .
(*As volunteer returns*) Still nothing, you're sure? You'd better go look once more.
(*As volunteer returns*) Nothing. Just one more time, check it again, would you mind?
(*As volunteer returns*) Still nothing, huh? Well, hmmm. Well, check it again, would you? Thanks.
(*As volunteer returns*) Did you find anything this time?

CHILD: No.

L: Nothing? OK. Well, what do you think, is it worth going one more time?
(*As volunteer returns*) You've been a good sport, you really have, thanks. You've looked six times but, well, seven is a very biblical number, would you consider going back one more time? Just once more . . . come on . . . (*The phrase "seven is a biblical number" is a prearranged cue for usher.*)
Hey, look at that! Where did that come from? Who would have thought . . . ?
(*To all the children*) Our friend has been acting a lot like Elijah this morning. Elijah told his servant to go look for something *seven times*: each time he came back Elijah told him to go look again. Why do you think God had Elijah tell his servant to do that? What was God trying to teach Elijah and his servant?

CHILDREN: Patience?

L: I think you're right. A very special kind of patience based on trust that God will take care of things. It seems as if God wants us to stick to it, to keep looking, to keep going back and looking and trusting as long as we're sent.

Let's have a prayer and ask God to help us be faithful, and to thank God for being faithful to us. (*Prayer.*)

GONE FISHIN'

Scripture: Luke 5:1-11
Focus: Over and over the Bible records miracle stories that involve God's action and people's reaction. An aspect of the miracle stories seems to be the connection between what God does and what we do in response to enjoy the fruit of God's grace. The focus of this sermon is to react to God's act.
Experience: To recreate, through imagination, being a disciple on the boat during the great catch of fish.
Arrangements: None are needed

LEADER: Let's meet out in the middle of the aisle. Good to see you all today. Let's sit down, and let's all pretend that we're sitting in a boat. (*Sit down and start rocking.*) We need somebody to be Jesus (*designate*) and somebody to be Peter (*designate*). Great!

A story in the Bible tells us that Peter and his partners had been out fishing all night and they hadn't caught a thing. So let's pretend first of all that you've been fishing all night, throwing the net out and pulling the net back in (*have children use arm motions to imitate this action*), throwing the net out, pulling it back in, over and over again, but you didn't catch any fish. Finally Peter and his partners came back to shore and got out of the boat. (*Stand.*)

Now, Jesus was out teaching and he borrowed Peter's boat to teach from because there were so many people on the shore. Peter and his friends were tired and frustrated, but they listened to Jesus while they cleaned their nets. When Jesus finished teaching, he said to Peter, "Put out into the deep water and let down your nets for a catch." (*Locate "Jesus" and have child repeat words to that effect.*)

CHILD: Put out into the deep water and let down your nets for a catch.

L: Good. And Peter said, "We have worked all night long but have caught nothing. Yet if you say so, I will let down the nets." (*Locate "Peter" and have child repeat words to that effect.*)

CHILD: We've worked all night long but haven't caught anything, but if you say so I will let down the nets.

L: Good! So Peter, you get back into the boat. You and your partners get back into the deep water and throw the nets out once more (*have children throw*), but *this* time there are all kinds of fish in the nets! (*Excitedly!*) The nets are so full it looks like they're going to burst. You really have to use your muscles to pull them in! Oh boy are they heavy, look at all those fish, fish are everywhere, all around you, and you're straining to pull in the net . . .

c: I got a fish!

L: You got a BIG fish! Whew! Now you're really tired. Well . . . what do you think those men did next after they caught all those fish?

c: Ate 'em.

L: They ate them! Absolutely! And on top of that, a lot of those men decided that this Jesus was somebody they needed to follow, somebody whose disciple they needed to be. They had just heard him teaching and now he told them how to catch fish. In fact, Jesus told them that he would make them fish for people and not just for big ol' slimy fish. (*Laughter.*) Let's have a prayer and thank God for the way we're called to become disciples of Jesus. (*Prayer.*)

GOSPEL CHANGES

Scripture: Matthew 21:12-13

Focus: The gospels cause us to believe that Jesus was frequently unpopular with the religious establishment of his day because he dared to suggest that God's Spirit might lead us to make changes. The focus of this sermon is the fact of change as part of the Christian life.

Experience: To notice that something is out of place in the church, and to hear the story of Jesus cleansing the temple. You may or may not want to include the final experience of having the children return to a different seat somewhere in the church and then having their families come and join them, the purpose of which is to bring about change in the usually predictable seating patterns, and thus interaction, of people in a church.

Arrangements: The catalyst for this sermon is something that is noticeably out of place in the church. It may be a table, a chair, the baptismal font, or something else moved to a location that is clearly "wrong." Be sure ushers and others responsible for worship know not to move it back!

LEADER: Good morning! Will the children please meet me in the side aisle? (*As children assemble*) There's a change in the church today, what is it?

CHILDREN: The cross!

L: The cross is in the middle of the aisle! How do you suppose it got here?

C: Don't know. Somebody moved it.

L: Somebody has moved it. Do you think it's a change for the better? Do you think that this is a good place for the cross to be?

C: Yes. No.

L: Well, before we decide on that let me tell you a story; some of you may already know it. One day Jesus was in Jerusalem and decided to go into the temple. Inside there were people exchanging normal money for a special kind of money you could only use in the temple, and other people selling things, and in general it was noisy and seemed more like a store than a church. Do you know what Jesus did?

C: He got mad.

L: He did get mad, and he made some changes! But then some of the ministers in the temple got mad at Jesus, because they didn't want any changes. They wanted things to be just the way they were. What do you think, do you think God wants us to make changes sometimes?

C: Yes. Maybe. Depends on if you're doing something bad.

L: I think you're right. It seems that God wants us to change if we're doing something bad, or if we could just do something that's good even better. Well, what about this cross? Do you think we should change it back to where it was? Or do you think we should leave it here as a reminder, at least for today, that sometimes God wants us to make a change.

C: Leave it!

L: OK, well, let's have a prayer and thank God for changes. (*Prayer.*)

THE ACCUSED

Scripture: Mark 14:53-65
Focus: The suffering of our Lord Jesus Christ is a difficult subject even for adults, yet it is an important part of our faith. The focus of

this sermon is to link a "created emotion" of fleeting panic to the much more real and lasting feelings experienced by Jesus. **Experience:** To feel, directly or vicariously, what it is to be falsely accused, by staging a situation in which one of the children is accused of stealing something around the church. To cue the congregation that it was really just a setup, we accused a seventy-pound boy of stealing the three-hundred-pound church bell! The theft of a piano would communicate the same signal. **Arrangements:** This children's sermon takes some careful handling in choosing the child to be singled out. In almost all groups there is generally one among the older children who is fairly self-confident and outspoken. A call to his or her parents to explain what it is you plan to do and to get their permission is essential. It will also help make sure that the child will be present in worship. Two other adults are needed, one to make the accusation (in this case, Ferris, chairperson of the Buildings and Grounds Committee) and the other to assure everyone that the accusation is false (in this case, Victor, the other minister in the church). These persons, well known to the congregation as deacons or others who would know about the church's physical plant, will need to be contacted ahead of time and given their cues. A brief rehearsal sometime before worship might be a good idea. Other deacons or ushers might be involved as below for dramatic effect.

LEADER: Good to see everybody! I want to share with you this morning about something that happened to Jesus. Jesus was crucified, he was killed on a cross, because while he was in court some men lied about him. Since Jesus didn't break any laws, they had to make something up that he did. This is what it says in Mark 14:55-56: "the chief priests and the whole Jewish Supreme Court were trying to find something against Jesus that would be sufficient to condemn him to death. But their efforts were in vain. Many false witnesses volunteered, but they contradicted each other."

USHER: (*shouting*) Ferris, wait, you can't go in there!

FERRIS: (*Bursting in from the back of the church*) I have to get this taken care of right now.

L: Ferris, what are you doing?

FERRIS: (*Arriving at the front of the church*) Someone has stolen the church bell.

L: What?

FERRIS: That's right, someone has stolen the church bell, and I know who it was. It was Kevin. (*He points at the "culprit," which elicits laughter from the congregation.*)

L: Kevin! Kevin stole the church bell?

KEVIN: I didn't!

L: Kevin! This is an outrage! What do you have to say for yourself, Kevin? Guilty or not guilty?

KEVIN:: I didn't do it!

L: (*Still sounding unconvinced by Kevin's protests*) I just can't believe that you would do something like that and then try and get out of it!

VICTOR: Listen everybody, there's been some mistake: the church bell hasn't been stolen.

FERRIS: Oh!

L: Oh, well, thanks anyway, Ferris (*laughter as Ferris leaves*). Sorry, Kevin, no hard feelings, OK? Well, that was a little exciting . . . what were we talking about just before all that happened?

CHILDREN: (*Let them work on remembering*) The people who killed Jesus.

L: That's right, the trial of Jesus, somebody said he did something that he didn't do. How do you think Jesus felt about that? Well, Kevin, how did you feel just now when Ferris said you'd stolen the church bell? Did it make you feel mad, and maybe sad, too?

KEVIN: (*Nods.*)

L: I bet that's the way Jesus felt too, but he didn't do anything about it and he didn't have anybody stand up for him and tell the truth. All he could do was to trust God, that somehow everything would work out for good. Well, let's have a prayer and thank God that we can trust God to take care of us when everybody seems against us, and that God was with Jesus when he went through those difficult days. (*Prayer.*)

TO ALL LANDS

Scripture: Matthew 28:18-20
Season/Sunday: Mission Sunday
Focus: The Great Commission given by Jesus in Matthew 28 makes it clear that we are to go into all the world to share the word of God. There are at least two parts to developing this skill: knowing the message and practicing its delivery.

Experience: To learn the message of God's love and to practice telling others about it by sending children to different "lands" in the church.

Arrangements: None are needed, but you may want to review the languages below and decide which you will use in your setting. You may even want to create some new ones!

LEADER: Good morning, good to see you. Did you know that there's a story in the Bible that tells us the very last words Jesus said before he went up into heaven? A story in the book of Matthew tells us that the last thing Jesus did was to tell his disciples to go out on a mission into all the world and make disciples by telling people all about the things Jesus did. How would you like to go out on a mission today, taking the message of Jesus Christ to the ends of the church?

CHILDREN: Yeah!

L: OK, does anybody here speak Balconese?

C: (*Tentatively raised hand.*)

L: Great! Why don't you go on up to the balcony and tell the gospel to as many people up there as you can—say to them "Jesus loves you." Next, does anybody here know any Transeptonian? Good, all of you head over to the transept over there and tell them the gospel, "Jesus loves you." Next we need a good many folk who speak Congregationese . . . super, all of you spread out into the congregation and spread the gospel to as many as you can. Only a few left . . . let's see, you wouldn't happen to know Choirish would you? You do? Great! Head on over to the choir and let them in on the good news.

All right, missionaries, time to come on back for a furlough. (*As children reassemble*) Did you have any problems?

C: No.

L: I'm glad. Being a missionary can be hard sometimes, but there's great reward too. Because by telling people that Jesus loves them, we not only are doing what Jesus wants us to do, but we also help people. Let's have a prayer and thank God for trusting us with this important work. (*Prayer.*)

SPEAK UP

Scripture: Acts 4:13-21

Focus: Worship is the first priority of the church, but it sometimes can get lost amidst all of our good intentions. Peter's words to the Sanhedrin provide a corrective to them and to us.

Experience: To have "business as usual" in worship interrupted by praise and proclamation. In this sermon the choir erupts in singing, right in the middle of what starts out as a rather boring children's sermon!

Arrangements: The choir needs to know that they will be singing one verse from a hymn of praise, and know their cue. The choir director (in our case, Mr. Clark) should also be supplied with a copy of the script and a microphone if necessary.

LEADER: Good morning! Let me tell you a story about two men from the Bible named Peter and John. You've probably heard of them before. Peter and John were in a city telling people about Jesus Christ, teaching and preaching the gospel, and the city council, the leaders of the city, said, "You're not supposed to do that. You have to stop teaching about Jesus Christ." And Peter and John said, "Whether it is right in God's sight to listen to you rather than to God, you must judge." So this morning we're going to have a meeting like the city council meeting. This meeting will please come to order. All those in favor please say "Aye." (*This is the choir's cue to begin singing. The choir sings one stanza of a hymn of praise such as "Praise to the Lord, the Almighty."*)

L: (*Trying to interrupt, showing surprise*) Uh, Mr. Clark? Mr. Clark . . . (*as verse comes to an end*) Mr. Clark, uh, that was very nice, but I'm trying to conduct a meeting here . . . what's going on?

MR. CLARK: We're doing what God has called us to do—we're singing praises.

L: Well, OK, that's nice, but we're having a meeting. You have to stop, it's not right for you to do that.

MR. CLARK: We just can't stop . . . God has called us to praise, and it's the right thing to do. We must listen to God and obey this call to worship.

L: (*To children*) What do you think, has he got a good argument? It sounds pretty good to me. If that's what God has called you

to do, it must be the right thing. Well, I'll make a deal with you: let me have a prayer with these young people and then while they're dismissing you can continue praising God, OK?
MR. CLARK: That'll be fine!
L: Let's pray, thanking God for the importance of worship, and then the choir can get on with praising. (*Prayer.*)

PRISONERS FOR CHRIST

Scripture: Acts 16:25-34
Focus: The God we worship is a powerful God. But that power is often found in connection with human trust. In many cases it seems that God chooses to bind divine power with human faith and obedience. The focus of this sermon is to experience God's power and human faith by reliving a biblical story which shows their connection.
Experience: To act out the scene of Paul and Silas in prison by creating a jail (using members of the congregation) and an imaginary earthquake.
Arrangements: None are needed, unless you care to mention in the bulletin that some people will be asked to stand, form a circle around the children who will gather in the aisle, and join hands to simulate a prison wall.

LEADER: Good morning! Let's meet in the middle of the church in the aisle. Everybody have a seat on the floor. Today we're looking at the story in Acts about Paul and Silas being in prison. We need three volunteers, one to be Paul, one to be Silas, and one to be a jailer. (*Assign parts.*)

(*To the congregation*) If you are sitting at the end of the pew on either side of us here, would you stand; and if you are in the pew just behind us there and just in front, move across and then everyone join hands, so that we end up with "prison walls" encircling us.

Now, where's our jailer? You need to be outside of the prison walls. OK, it seems as though Paul and Silas, because they were preaching about Jesus Christ, made some people unhappy and got themselves thrown in prison. Now it says in Acts that Paul and Silas—where are Paul and Silas?—were singing hymns and praying . . . let's see, Paul and Silas, why don't you fold your hands and sing "Jesus Loves Me." (*Children start singing softly.*) And suddenly there was a great earthquake, so that the foundations of the prison were shaken. So everybody inside is shaking (*make sure children shake*), oh my what an earthquake, and the walls, the walls were shaking (*make very sure the walls shake*). And immediately all the doors were opened and everyone's chains were unfastened. So, people across the front here, be our door, and you swing open, and everyone stand up because your chains are unfastened.

OK, now what would you do if you were in prison and your chains came off and the doors flew open?

CHILDREN: Get out!

L: You'd get out, absolutely! But you know what? Paul and Silas didn't do that. Here's what happened. The jailer woke up (*wake up jailer, indicate stretching, yawning*) and wondered, What's going on? Say, "Oh my goodness! The prison doors are open. This is terrible. I'm going to kill myself."

JAILER: (*Repeating words to this effect*) Oh my goodness! The prison doors are open. I'm going to kill myself.

L: . . . because the jailer really thought that the prisoners had escaped, and he knew he was in trouble. But Paul—where's Paul?—Paul said, "Don't do that! We're all here!"

PAUL: (*Repeating words to this effect*) Don't do that, we're all here!

L: So the jailer came running into the prison (*jailer moves into prison*) and was amazed to find all the people there, and so he said to Paul, "What must I do to be saved?"

JAILER: What must I do to be saved?

L: And Paul said to the jailer, "Believe in Jesus Christ."

PAUL: Believe in Jesus Christ.

L: Good. And because Paul and Silas trusted God and stayed in prison a new Christian was made and the jailer was baptized with all his family.

Let's have a prayer and thank God for the faith of Paul and Silas and for the mighty power of God. (*Prayer.*)

CHURCH YEAR

PREPARING THE WAY

Scripture: Matthew 3:1-3
Season/Sunday: Advent
Focus: Advent is a time of preparation. According to John the Baptist, part of that preparation is "making straight" for the coming of Christ. There are many possible meanings for the phrase "make straight," but essentially they all come down to getting things in right, clean, and good order for the coming of the Lord.
Experience: To clean up the church as one aspect of "preparing" and "making straight" that we can experience. Short of leveling a local mountain, this is a good way for children to understand something of what John meant.
Arrangements: Have some rags, brooms, feather dusters available.

LEADER: Good morning! (*With urgency and excitement throughout*) We have so much to do! Busy, busy, busy!! Come on, hurry, we've got lots of things to do! It's a busy time. You know what, there are only eleven days left, and do you know what that means?
CHILDREN: Twelve more . . .
L: Twelve? OK, that's good. That gives us one more . . . she's counting! Twelve days to do what?
C: Celebrate? Go shopping?
L: I thought you might say that, but Christmas shopping is the least of our worries—we have to *prepare*! We have to get ready. John the Baptist said to prepare the way of the Lord. (*To one of the children*) Here, stand up and take this broom and start sweeping over there, we've got to prepare. (*With urgency*) Here's the broom, hurry, get going, sweep, we've got to get ready! (*Distribute rags to some of the children, have them start dusting the pews, communion table, pulpit, and other areas.*) We've got to get ready, to be prepared for a special visitor. Dust, sweep, clean! Here, take a rag and get started over there . . . Busy, busy, hurry, get going, we've got to get ready, we've got things to do! We've got preparations to make, here, start cleaning over there, we've got things to get ready!

OK, time's up. May I have the rags back please, time's up, we've got to finish. Oh, such a busy time, such a busy time. Good job.

It is a busy time, isn't it? And we have to prepare and get ready and we've hardly just begun. Advent is a time for preparing. It's a busy time, but we need to be sure to take time to prepare, to get ready, to make straight the crooked, and to get ready for a very special visitor . . . who's that?

c: Jesus.

L: Jesus. Let's all hold hands and thank God for sending us Jesus, and to ask for help in taking time to be quiet, to take a moment in the midst of all our other busy preparations to prepare for the coming of Jesus. (*Prayer.*)

FOR CRYING OUT LOUD

Scripture: Mark 1:1-3
Season/Sunday: Advent
Focus: An undeniable aspect of John's ministry was the enthusiastic proclamation of the good news of Christ's coming. Our proclamation should be no less enthusiastic.
Experience: To grant "permission" to the children to make such a proclamation by shouting in church.
Arrangements: None are needed.

LEADER: Come on down! Good to see you all today! How many of you like to yell and shout?

CHILDREN: (*Lots of raised hands.*)

L: How many of you have ever gotten in trouble for yelling and shouting?

c: (*Lots of raised hands.*)

L: Uh huh . . . at home maybe, or even maybe at church sometimes? Well, I want to tell you a story today about a young man whose name was John. John was very excited about something that was about to happen. In fact, he got so excited that he wanted to shout about it. John knew that he'd better not shout at home because he'd get into trouble, so he went far away, way out into the desert, and he started yelling and shouting out there because he was so excited and happy. Do you know what he was shouting? He was shouting, "Jesus is coming!" as loudly as he could!

Advent, the season we are in right now, is all about preparing and proclaiming—shouting about the coming of Jesus. How would you like to shout right now in church? Let's all shout, as

loudly as we can, "Jesus is coming!" OK, ready? On three—
one, two, three . . .
c: Jesus is coming! (*Shouting could be done again with congregation involved.*)
L: Amen! That was beautiful! We may never get that chance again in church! Let's pray and thank God that Jesus is coming. (*Prayer.*)

WAITING

Scripture: Luke 2:25-32
Season/Sunday: Advent
Focus: One aspect of Advent is waiting for the coming of Jesus. Waiting serves to heighten our expectation of the fulfillment of Christ's coming.
Experience: To wait long enough to get a sense of that heightened expectation.
Arrangements: None are needed.

LEADER: (*Silence. The key to this children's sermon is to keep expectations up through two minutes of silence! At first you might just sit, then begin to use gestures, such as holding your face in your hands or looking at your watch to communicate that you are waiting. Then begin.*) What's the hardest part about Christmas?
CHILDREN: Waiting!
L: Waiting. Seems like it takes forever, doesn't it? Well, you know the season of the Christian year right now is called Advent, and part of Advent means waiting. Waiting and waiting and waiting. Who are we waiting for?
c: Santa Claus.
L: (*After regaining composure*) I suppose I walked right into that one! Who else are we waiting for?
c: Jesus.
L: Thank you. Jesus. Advent is the time that we wait for Jesus. It's kind of hard for us in the year 19___ to really imagine waiting for Jesus because we know Jesus has already come. But the people waiting on the first Christmas, they were just waiting, and they

didn't really know what for. In Advent we take time to think about what life would be like without Jesus, what it would be like if Jesus hadn't come yet, to help us appreciate more the fact that he did come!

Let's pray and thank God that we know that at the end of our time of waiting, Jesus has come. (*Prayer.*)

TURN

Scripture: John 1:19-28
Season/Sunday: Advent
Focus: One theme of Advent has to do with the meaning of repentance as announced by John the Baptist. One meaning of repentance is "to turn," away from our sin, ourselves, and even from John himself, to Jesus Christ.
Experience: To be surprised by the appearance of John the Baptist.
Arrangements: Someone is needed to come in and stand as John the Baptist at the back of the church (or in the balcony) after the children have gathered in their usual place. Costuming would be helpful, perhaps even a hooded robe to focus attention on the message rather than the messenger.

LEADER: How is everybody today? Good to see you! Can you remember the church season we're in right now?
CHILDREN: Christmas?
B: Christmas . . . and Advent, that time right before Christmas. One of the people we think a lot about during Advent is John the Baptist. John the Baptist was a preacher who lived out in the desert and wore strange clothes and ate strange food, like grasshoppers . . . and he had a strange message, too. While he was out in the desert, John the Baptist would say things like . . .
JOHN THE BAPTIST: (*From the back of the sanctuary or balcony, with a deep booming voice and arms raised for dramatic effect*) Repent!
L: Look, it's John the Baptist. (*Yelling to visitor*) Mr. Baptist, sir. We are honored by your being here and your message to us. But I'm not sure we understand your message. Can you tell us what "repent" means?

JOHN THE BAPTIST: Turn.

L: Turn. Well, OK, let's turn. What do you see? (*John the Baptist should leave as soon as the children have turned back around.*)

C: Cross . . . Communion table . . . Advent candles . . . Bible.

L: Good! And those things remind us of somebody, who's that?

C: Jesus!

L: Jesus, that's right. They remind us of Jesus. So John . . . John left! Well, I guess he doesn't want us thinking about him, he wants us to turn and think about Jesus during this time of year, and that's what Advent is for. Let's all hold hands and thank God for sending John the Baptist to give us that message. (*Prayer.*)

A THIEF IN THE NIGHT

Scripture: 1 Thessalonians 5:1-11

Season/Sunday: Advent

Focus: God in Christ surprises us by coming to us in many unexpected ways—a baby in a manger, a man on a cross, a thief in the night—all reminding us to trust in God's leading and God's grace.

Experience: To have the children's sermon interrupted by a thief who comes in to the church to "steal Jesus."

Arrangements: You will need to have someone dressed, rehearsed, and cued to be the thief. A "Lone Ranger" type mask and a trenchcoat can serve as costume, and the cue is an agreed-upon phrase. You may also want to have other effects, such as the banging of a door somewhere in the general area of the thief's entry, other noises, and perhaps even a dimming of the lights. Be sure to alert other worship participants what is happening; I forgot to do so, and there was some genuine concern on their part when the lights went out!

LEADER: Good to see everyone today! Let's talk about surprises. Have any of you ever gotten surprised?

CHILDREN: Yes.

(*Door bangs; leader glances that way, but continues.*)

L: OK, tell us about a time when you were surprised.

C: (*Relates incident.*)

(*Another loud noise is heard; leader responds with facial concern.*)

L: Well, that would be a surprise! (*Cue for lights to go out.*) Hmmm. I'd better go check this out. (*Investigate by opening door leading to area in which noises were heard earlier, and reveal the "thief."*) A thief! What do you want?

THIEF: I've come to steal Jesus!

L: Steal Jesus? (*To children*) Does he have to *steal* Jesus?

C: Noooo!

L: No, you don't have to steal Jesus. The surprise of Christmas is that Jesus comes as an unexpected gift for us. Would you like to come and worship with us and hear more about it?

THIEF: Well, sure, I guess so. (*Thief takes seat in congregation.*)

L: Wow, wasn't that something! Let's have a prayer and thank God that we get surprised by the gift of Jesus Christ at Christmas time. (*Prayer.*)

THE CHRISTMAS STORY

Scripture: Matthew 1:18-21, 24-25 (RSV)
Season/Sunday: Christmas Sunday
Focus: The incarnation is a mysterious and awe-inspiring event. But it is also a flesh-and-blood event. One of the challenges of the Christmas story is to keep both aspects in view.
Experience: To recreate and be a part of the Christmas story in such a way as to enjoy its flesh-and-blood reality, and perhaps also gain a sense of its mysterious qualities.
Arrangements: This children's sermon is a telling of the story in Matthew 1:18-21, 24-25, using as many persons to help tell it as possible. Begin by explaining to everyone that when certain words are said a response is indicated. Then proceed to describe the key words and their response, beginning and ending with the children's parts. Lead each group in practicing its part. Perhaps the choir can practice briefly before worship or during the choir's regular rehearsal.

LEADER: Good morning. This morning we're going to be in a story, the story found in the first chapter of Matthew. Everybody has a part in the story when I read certain words.

Children (*divided into three groups*):
  "Jesus"—da, ta da (like trumpets)
  "Mary"—ahhh (sigh sweetly)
  "Joseph"—hey Joe! (*deep voice*)
Congregation (*divided into two groups*):
  "Holy Spirit"—whoossh (*sound like wind*)
  "dream"—snore
Choir:
  "angel"— first six words from "Angels We Have Heard On High"

L: OK, here's the story!

"Now the birth of Jesus (*pause*) Christ took place in this way. When his mother Mary (*pause*) had been betrothed to Joseph (*pause*), before they came together Mary (*pause*) was found to be with child of the Holy Spirit (*pause*); and her husband Joseph (*pause*), being a just man and unwilling to put Mary (*pause*) to shame, resolved to divorce her quietly. But as Joseph (*pause*) considered this, behold, an angel (*pause*) of the Lord appeared to him in a dream (*pause*), saying, "Joseph (*pause*), son of David, do not fear to take Mary (*pause*) your wife, for that which is conceived in her is of the Holy Spirit (*pause*); she will bear a son, and you shall call his name Jesus (*pause*), for he will save his people from their sins. . . .

"When Joseph (*pause*) woke from his dream (*pause*), he did as the angel (*pause*) of the Lord commanded him; he took Mary (*pause*) as his wife, but knew her not until she had borne a son; and he called his name Jesus (*pause*)."

Let's have a prayer and thank God for the excitement of Jesus' birth. (*Prayer.*)

OUT OF THE ASHES

Scripture: Job 42:1-6
Season/Sunday: Lent
Focus: Lent is a season for repentance and sorrow. In some traditions it is common to burn the palms from Palm Sunday and use the ash to

mark the sign of the cross on the forehead on Ash Wednesday, as a sign of penitence and confession at the beginning of Lent.
Experience: To trace the form of a cross on the child's forehead or on the back of the child's hand.
Arrangements: You will need some ash in a bowl. A little goes a long way!

LEADER: Good morning, how's everybody doing? Who can tell me what season this is right now?
CHILDREN: Winter.
L: Winter, that's right. You know the Christian year has seasons too—does anybody know what season it is in the Christian year? That's a little bit harder question . . . Well, we started last December with the season of Advent, that was right before Christmas. We had Advent, and then Christmas, and then Epiphany. And now, right before Easter, we're in a season that is called "Lent." Not, lint, not like lint from the clothes dryer. Lent. Lent is a time for repentance. That's a big word, but basically repentance means being sorry, being sorry for the things that we've done that we shouldn't have done. In the Old Testament, back a long time ago, when people were sorry for what they'd done they would take some ashes and put them on themselves to show that they were sorry. Now, some churches still do this—they take ash and put it on a person's forehead. That was last Wednesday, and we call it Ash Wednesday.

Well, I brought some ashes today and I'd like to give you all a little bit of ash in the form of a cross on your forehead (*or on the back of the hand*). You don't have to do it if you don't want, but it doesn't hurt. Just a little bit of ash to remember that this is the season of Lent, a time of being sorry and that it's a time of preparing for Easter. (*Enjoy this intimate time one-on-one with the children.*)

THE TRIUMPHAL ENTRY
Scripture: John 12:12-13
Season/Sunday: Palm Sunday

Focus: There is a tension between the triumphal entry of Jesus on Palm Sunday and the terrible pain of his cross later in the week. Since not all children will participate in Maundy Thursday or Good Friday services, the story of Jesus and the cross can get lost. Palm Sunday can provide an introduction to the cross by showing it to be a continuation of Jesus' entry into Jerusalem.

Experience: By using the imagination, to be present at the triumphal entry of Jesus, and to follow his journey on to the cross.

Arrangements: Supplying the children with palm braches will add to the event, especially if the branches can be left in the aisle at the end of the sermon. Also, two ushers will need to be alert to the cue for opening the doors.

LEADER: Come on down here and have a seat. Good to see you all! We're going to pretend today that we're in Jerusalem, and it's the day that Jesus is coming to town. We've heard about him, we've heard that he's coming, and we've decided to go out onto the street that he's coming into town on in order to meet him (*the aisle will be the "street"*). Let's all stand up and go out and line the street here. Come on down here and everybody stand by the end of a pew, so we are on both sides of the street. (*It may take a minute or two to get children in place.*) We're lining the street because we've heard that Jesus is coming, and everybody has a palm branch (*either real or pretend*). Here, pick this one up. (*Pretending to pick up palm branches and hand them to the children.*)

(*Excitedly*) OK, we know that Jesus is coming, and we've come out onto the street, and we're getting excited because we know he's coming, and we're looking down the street, (*back toward doors leading into sanctuary*) and suddenly (*"And suddenly" is the cue for ushers to open doors at back of sanctuary in one swift, dramatic movement. Of course no one is to be seen in the narthex; the opening doors are the representation of Jesus' entry.*) There's Jesus! (*make sure that you have positioned yourself at the chancel end of the "street," that is, farthest away from the opening doors and thus behind the children as they look back toward the doors, so that there is no confusion of your being Jesus!*) Here he comes! (*Keep excitement up.*) Everybody wave your palms and say "Hosanna!" Let's all say it . . .

CHILDREN: Hosanna! Hosanna!

L: Hosanna! And you lay down your palms on the street in front of Jesus. And here he comes, and you're still saying "Hosanna!"

c: Hosanna!

l: Here he comes, and he's passing right by us, here he comes, here he comes . . . (*quieter now*) . . . and where is he going? (*Point to a cross somewhere in the chancel area.*) He's going to the cross. (*Long pause to let this sink in.*)

Let's all hold hands and have a prayer thanking God for the excitement we feel about the coming of Jesus, and asking God to be with us in the coming week as we are also sad knowing that Jesus is going to the cross. (*Prayer.*)

MARY'S STORY

Scripture: Matthew 28:1-10
Season/Sunday: Easter Sunday
Focus: The resurrection is a difficult concept to grasp, even for adults. A more accessible reality for children may be the excitement of someone who says they have seen the empty tomb.
Experience: To be a disciple of Jesus and to be present to hear of Jesus' resurrection.
Arrangements: A young woman willing to act out the part of Mary. She will need to memorize the basic flow of the conversation (although some ad lib is fine) and give the part credible excitement. A rehearsal together would probably help, as would appropriate dress. Be sure to consider amplification.

LEADER: How you doing? Good to see you! Everybody's looking good this morning in their spring colors. Let's pretend this morning that we are the disciples of Jesus, and that we're sitting in the upper room early Sunday morning. We're together but we're kind of scared, and we're kind of lonely and afraid, because we know that Friday our Lord and Master Jesus Christ was crucified. We're not quite sure what we're going to do next. Let's see . . . how about if I'm Peter, and would you (*to one of the children next to you*) be John? Good. And would you (*to child on the other side*) be James? Great.

(*Sigh.*) John, are you sad like I am this morning? What about you James, are you lonely like I am? Yes, yes, I know. James, your mother, Mary, and the other Mary, Mary Magdalene, went to the grave of Jesus this morning. That seemed kind of a dangerous thing to me. I'm not sure why she did that . . . (*Cue for Mary to come running down the aisle from the narthex.*) Why look! Here comes Mary Magdalene now. She's running, do you think the Roman guards are after her?

MARY: Peter! Peter!

L: Mary, Mary—what's the matter?

MARY: Peter, James, John, all of you, listen! He's alive! He's alive!

L: Mary, calm down, catch your breath, take just a minute now. What is it you're saying?

MARY: Peter, all of you, Jesus is alive!

L: (*Shaking head in despair*) Mary, Mary . . .

MARY: James, you must believe me. . . . I was with your mother. We went to the tomb and the earth shook and the great stone was rolled away, and an angel of the Lord appeared and told us that Jesus wasn't there. Then the angel showed us the empty grave and told us to come back and tell all of you that Jesus isn't dead, he's alive!

L: Mary, I can't believe it. I'm disappointed, I can't believe that you would come here and make up a story like this.

MARY: I'm not making it up. We saw him, with our own eyes, as we were leaving!

L: You, you say you saw Jesus?

MARY: Yes! And he said to us, "Do not be afraid, but go and tell my friends to meet me in Galilee."

L: (*To disciples*) What do you think? This is too good to be true. This is . . . unbelievable! What do you think, should we believe, *dare* we believe this exciting news? Yes! Let's believe it! And let's go and meet Jesus in Galilee. Let's hold hands and have a prayer of thanksgiving to God that this great thing has been done. (*Prayer.*)

ASCENSION

Scripture: Acts 1:6-11
Season/Sunday: Ascension Sunday (this same format could be used to introduce any lesser known church holiday)

Focus: Ascension is the date in the Christian calendar that celebrates the return of Christ to the right hand of God, reclaiming his title as sovereign Lord of the universe.

Experience: To involve the congregation in Christian education, reminding them of their promise made at a child's baptism or dedication by asking them to define the meaning and purpose of this date in the church year.

Arrangements: None are needed

LEADER: Good morning! How's everybody? Today is a day in the church calendar that we call Ascension Sunday. That's a big word, isn't it? Ascension. Can everybody say "Ascension"?

CHILDREN: 'Cension.

L: Ascension Sunday. How about if we have a little fun with the congregation this morning? Let's go and ask people in the congregation why Ascension Sunday is important. You can go ask your mom or dad or ask somebody who you don't know, go ask the choir, anybody; then we'll come back and hear what everybody had to say. (*Children disperse.*) For the first time, those of you who sit in the back might be glad . . . ! (*Children return.*)

OK, what kind of answers did you get?

C: Nothing. Nobody knows. 'Cause Christ went back to heaven.

L: Well, Ascension Sunday is an important day because Christ went back to heaven, that's a good answer. Jesus Christ went back to heaven, and that's important because in doing that Jesus Christ became Lord of all the universe. That means Jesus is in charge over everything, he is King over everything. So we celebrate Ascension Sunday to remind us that Christ is Lord of everything from his heavenly throne.

Well, thank you for helping to test the congregation! Let's have a prayer and thank God for making Jesus Christ King of creation, and ask that we might better worship him as Lord. (*Prayer.*)

IN THEIR OWN TONGUE

Scripture: Acts 2:5-12
Season/Sunday: Pentecost

Focus: One aspect of Pentecost is as an event in the life of the church that leads to worship and that is inclusive of a diversity of peoples.

Experience: To use our voices to explore the variety of ways God is praised in creation.

Arrangements: None are needed

LEADER: Good morning, how's everybody? Let me ask you a question . . . what kind of a sound does a duck make?

CHILDREN: Quack, quack.

L: OK, what does a frog say?

C: Ribbit!

L: That's right! What sound does a rabbit make?

C: Hop.

L: A hop? Well, that is a sound, I guess! There's always one! (*This was a trick question that tricked back! If children don't have an answer you can supply "Rabbits wiggle their nose, like this . . . everybody wiggle your nose."*) Why do you think God made all these different sounds? Why didn't he just make one, like "Blaphhh"? Well, maybe all these different sounds glorify God—that means that all these different sounds make God happy. It seems like God likes all these different sounds—quacks and ribbits and chirps and even hops—and that's why we have so many, to glorify God, to praise God, each one in its own way. Well, what kind of sounds do people make? Do people say "Moo?"

C: (*Giggles.*) No!

L: What sounds do we make?

C: Words?

L: Right! We say all different kinds of words, in all different kinds of languages, using all of our different voices—some high, some low (*use high and a low voice*), and we believe that all of those different voices glorify God, make God happy. Everybody has a sound, everybody has words, and God gave these sounds and words to us to make God happy with them. In fact, today is Pentecost Sunday, which is a holiday we celebrate in the life of the church to remind us that God wants to be praised and worshiped in all different languages and sounds. Well, what words do we have to glorify God? Could we say, "Praise God"?

C: Yes.

L: OK, let's all say that, first all the high voices, if you have a high voice (*demonstrate*) say "Praise God" as loud as you can . . .

c: Praise God!

L: OK! Now all the low voices . . .

c: Praise God!

L: Congregation, you try it too. (*Go through high voices and low voices, and have them do it loudly.*) Great!

Let's have a prayer and thank God that there are so many different sounds and voices to give God glory, and that each one is beautiful to God who created them. (*Prayer.*)

ALL THE SAINTS

Scripture: Hebrews 12:1-2; 1 Peter 2:9-10
Season/Sunday: Sunday nearest November 1, All Saints' Day
Focus: One aspect of All Saints' Day is a celebration of the priesthood of all believers who are saints (fully forgiven) in God's eyes. Central to this celebration is the Christian belief that every person has a special gift for use in the body of Christ and can minister to others.
Experience: To meet persons of all ages in the life and work of the church.
Arrangements: Decide on six or so people, young and old, men and women, whom you want to introduce in the course of this sermon. Call them in advance to be sure of their willingness to come forward. Be sure they understand the nature and purpose of the children's sermon as in the introduction below.

LEADER: Good morning, hope everyone is fine today. Are you fine? Fine! I've got a question for you . . . what's a saint?

CHILDREN: Someone holy?

L: Right, it can mean someone who has lived life in a holy way. Well, did you know we have some saints right here in the church? These people might not talk about themselves that way, and they certainly wouldn't think of themselves as any more holy than anybody else, but the Bible says that we are all holy, we are all saints, because of what Jesus has done for us. And the people I have in mind are saints because they work for good in lots of ways that you and I never even see. Saints are basically shy people, but I've asked some of our saints to come forward this morning so you can meet them.

Here's Jay Cummins. He works in the Youth Club Program, helping in the kitchen every single week, so that the rest of us can eat.

Charlotte Safrit is an officer in the Senior High Fellowship and helps the senior highs as they serve the church and the community in service projects like the CROP Walk.

Larry Kramer is in the choir and also helps coach the junior high basketball team.

Ann Whaley is a very quiet worker in the church but very faithfully teaches in Bethel, serves as a deacon, and helps lead her Sunday school class.

Bernie Wilcox is a woman of great faith whom you might not see up front very often but whose prayers are the fuel that helps keep the church glowing.

Ernest Jamison is one of the men who keeps this church from falling apart. He keeps the lights lit and the heaters hot and the doors from squeaking.

Olin Flow has been an inspiration to countless people over the years, through his faithfulness and through his firm belief in tithing, a belief that he has passed on to many in our church.

And behind all of these people is what?

c: The cross, the communion table, the Bible . . .

l: The cross, the communion table, the Bible . . . all of those things are their foundation, the things that allow them to do all the things they do. Let's have a prayer and thank God for these saints, for all the saints in the church, and for the power of Jesus Christ that helps us all. (*Prayer.*)

WORSHIP

GROWING UP IN CHURCH

Scripture: Ephesians 4:15-16

Focus: As we grow and change, our faith grows and changes too. While these changes can sometimes be challenging, we find comfort in knowing that we keep moving in the same direction and toward a certain goal.

Experience: To move from the back of the church toward the front using the different forms of movement through the human life cycle.

Arrangements: If the church uses a baptismal font and it can be moved, move it down the aisle almost to the back of the church. Also, you will need a cross (or some other symbol depicting Christ), whether in a window or as part of the church architecture or furnishings. If the baptismal font cannot be moved, have the children meet at the back anyway in order to use the aisle as the "road," returning during the course of the sermon toward the front of the church.

LEADER: Would the children come and meet me at the baptismal font? Good morning, good to see you today. We're going to go on a journey today—a faith journey—the journey that we take through our lives. Most of us were baptized as babies, and that's a good place to begin a faith journey. But we've got to move on from there: how do babies move?

CHILDREN: Crawl.

L: They crawl, right. OK, let's all get down on the floor and crawl!

C: (*Giggles.*)

L: OK, after a while babies get older and become children. How do children move?

C: Walk?

L: Walk? Most children I know run! This may be the only chance you get to run in church . . . be careful you don't run over the person in front of you! Let's run! (*Run a short distance up the aisle, or let them run up the aisle and back to you.*) OK, as we continue on our faith journey we go from being children to what?

C: Grown-ups.

L: Right, and how do grown-ups move?

C: Walk.

L: Yeah, they're boring, they just walk along . . . so we'll walk along . . . And finally, grown-ups get older, maybe become grandparents, and how do grandparents move?

C: Slow.

L: Right, slow, maybe even a little bent over. So let's all move like grandparents. (*You should end up at the front of the church.*) Good. Well, you know, there are all these different kinds of people in the church, and all these different ways of moving through the church, but all of us are moving in the same direction—toward (*point to cross*) Jesus Christ. He's the one we are all moving toward, and he's the one who is also with us on our journey. Let's have a prayer and thank God for being with us on our journey through life. (*Prayer.*)

WHAT DO YOU WANT TO BE WHEN YOU GROW UP?

Scripture: Ephesians 4:15-16
Focus: As we grow up we find that some things change while others remain constant. One of the constants is our faith. The focus of this sermon is that what we want to be when we grow up may change in terms of our profession, but remains constant in terms of our confession.
Experience: To name what we want to be when we grow up and to see those in the congregation who shared that same dream as children *but did not go on to do the work named.*
Arrangements: None are needed, but you may wish to put a note in the bulletin explaining that adults will be asked to stand (and remain standing) when a kind of work is called out that they at some time considered while growing up but did not pursue. If you have fewer than five or six children you might want to consider calling on older youth in the congregation (junior or senior highs) for their hoped-for vocational choice, and asking adults to stand as before.

LEADER: Everybody looks so bright-eyed today! That's good, because I want to ask you a question: Have you ever thought about what you want to be when you grow up? Has anyone ever asked you that?
CHILDREN: Yes!
L: Great! In just a minute I'm goint to ask each one of you what you think you want to be when you grow up. Congregation, when they tell us, I would like to invite any of you who at one time

in your life wanted to be that too, but ended up becoming something else, to stand. Do you understand? (*Explain again as necessary.*) OK, what do you want to be when you grow up?

c: A nurse.

L: Any onetime aspiring nurses in the congregation? Please stand up! Stay standing! Now you, what do you want to be when you grow up?

c: A football player.

L: I'll have to stand up on that one, anyone else? (*Continue until all children have spoken.*)

Now, I want you to look at all those people standing up out there. All of them wanted to do one thing for a living when they were growing up, but ended up doing something else. But do you know what, even though they grew up to *do* something else, they all grew up to *be* the same thing. All of them grew up to be Christians. That's something to think about, isn't it?

(*To the congregation*) After church you might want to get together to talk about your shared dreams with these bright-eyed children. Right now, let's have a prayer and thank God that no matter what we grow up to do, we can always grow up to be Christians. (*Prayer.*)

THE CROSS

Scripture: Colossians 2:13-14
Focus: Our sin is forgiven in Christ's act on the cross. This is a difficult but central truth of our faith. The focus of this sermon is to bring this truth from the abstract realm of words to an experience to be remembered.
Experience: To nail to the cross our IOU (I Owe You) to God. The IOUs represent what we "owe" God because we have sinned, what Paul calls the record that stands against us.
Arrangements: You will need a wooden cross (you may want to make a simple cross of two pieces of wood for this occasion), a hammer, a nail (getting the hole started beforehand can save your thumb!), paper, and a marker pen.

LEADER: Good morning! Let me read to you a little bit out of a letter from a man named Paul to some people called the Colossians. Paul talks about Jesus, "God made you alive together with him, when he forgave us all our trespasses, erasing the record that stood against us with its legal demands. He set this aside, nailing it to the cross."

Paul talks about a record that stands against us, something that we owe. Does anybody know what an IOU is? (*On a piece of paper write the letters IOU at the top with a marker pen while explaining.*) "I," "O," like I owe you something, "U." IOU. If I owed you some money, I would sign an IOU so we could both remember it. Well, the record that Paul talks about is like an IOU that we owe God because each one of us has sinned. I'm going to put my X on this paper to sign it and say, yes, I owe God because I've sinned. What if each one of us puts an X on this paper to represent all the things we ought not to have done that we owe God for? (*Pass paper around.*)

(*As paper goes around*) This doesn't mean that God keeps a list of all the things we do wrong, but at one time there was a kind of list. Paul tells us that when human beings were under the Law, under a whole set of rules, that there was a record kept. But when Jesus Christ came, Paul says, he took that list, that IOU and he did something very special with it—he nailed it to the cross. He nailed it to the cross so that all of our sins would be erased, forgiven, forgotten. I brought a cross for us to use, and a hammer and a nail, and we're going to nail this IOU to the cross. And once it's been nailed there we can just forget about it, because that's what God did. He said, "I forget about this IOU, it's nailed to the cross once and for all." So we don't have to worry about it anymore. I'll put one more big X on here for the entire congregation. (*Roll up paper and nail it to center of cross.*) In Jesus Christ we're all forgiven, and we don't have to worry about what we owe God anymore.

Let's all hold hands and thank God for forgetting what we owe and giving us this good news. (*Prayer.*)

IN-DOOR, OUT-DOOR

Scripture: Revelation 3:8
Focus: Worship and service are two sides of the same coin: we serve God in worship, we worship God in our service. The focus of this

sermon looks at the doors that are put before us for worship and service.

Experience: To examine the doors of the church and their twofold purpose.

Arrangements: None are needed, although a word to the ushers of your intended movement—to the back of the church (through the narthex) and to the main doors of the church—may help things go more smoothly.

LEADER: Good morning! Let's all meet at the doors. All the way back to the front doors of the church. How is everybody today? Good! Let me ask you a question. We're all in here, right? How did we get in here?

CHILDREN: We walked.

L: Walked where, walked through what?

C: The halls, the door.

L: The door, somebody said the door. Well, this is a door right here, isn't it? Let's look at this door (*open door(s) to the outside*) . . . it's a pretty day outside. Look at this door: is this door an in-door or an out-door?

C: Both.

L: Both. We came *in* a little while ago . . . what did we come in to do?

C: Pray, worship God, sing . . .

L: So we came in the in-door to do all those things, to worship God. Later we're going to go out this door, right? What will we go out the door to do?

C: Go home!

L: Go home! All right, well, I suppose that's true. Let's go out the door. (*Move outside—you may want to reserve this sermon for warm weather!*) One of the other things we'll do later on when we come out the door is tell all the people who haven't been inside with us all that we heard in there. Let's see, we heard that Jesus loves us, right? How about if we stand here and tell all the people who are out there, anybody who will listen to us, let's yell real loud, that Jesus loves us. Everybody get ready to yell, on three. One, two, three . . .

C: Jesus loves us!

L: That was great! Let's go back inside. Well now, every time we see a door we can think about it being both an in-door and an out-door. And you know what? Almost every door is one that we either come in to worship God or go out and tell other people about God's love. Let's have a prayer and thank God for this place and for the doors in our lives. (*Prayer.*)

WHERE IS GOD?

Scripture: Psalm 139:7-12
Focus: One of our beliefs is in God's omnipresence. While this is an abstract concept beyond the capabilities of most of our children, the focus of this sermon is to have fun with it and in doing so plant the seeds for later understanding.
Experience: To search the inside of the church for God.
Arrangements: None are needed.

LEADER: Good to see everyone today! I have a question to ask. Where is God?
CHILDREN: Up in the sky.
L: Up in the sky. Anywhere else? Is God here?
C: Yes. God is everywhere!
L: If God is everywhere then God is here too, right? Where?
C: Here!
L: Where?
C: Here!
L: Well, let's look and see if we can find out where God is here. Why don't some of us go look out in the pews, some of us need to go look in the choir, some might come up here. Maybe God is in the pulpit. (*Be sure to look in and around the pulpit, to help demystify that great bulk of furniture!*) Oh, maybe we will find God in the baptismal font . . . let's look in there. What do you think?
C: Too small.
L: Too small. OK, how about under the chairs over there? (*To children at back of sanctuary*) Did you find God back there? No? Did anybody check the choir . . . they look suspicious, better check 'em out. Somebody check over there underneath the piano, would you? Not there either? Well, OK, everybody come on back here. We'll just have to sit down again and think about this.

c: I know where God is . . . God is everywhere and invisible.
L: God is everywhere and invisible? I wish you'd said that earlier!
My, you are clever! That's exactly right. (*If a child doesn't say
that, ask questions and lead to that conclusion.*) God is here with
us, but not only just here but everywhere, all the time, and that
makes God pretty amazing.
c: God's beside you.
L: That's right! Well, let's talk to God and thank God for being
beside all of us and everywhere. (*Prayer.*)

THE INTERVIEW

Scripture: Psalm 122:1
Focus: Worship is a central part of the Christian life, and the joyous
sharing of why it is so central is, in turn, an important part of
evangelism. The focus of this sermon is to share an understanding of
what worship is all about.
Experience: To be part of a news interview about what goes on in
church. The children will pretend that they are coming out of church
and being met by a reporter (you or someone you have arranged) for
an interview about what went on inside.
Arrangements: You will want a hand-held microphone, a video
camera unit with someone to be the camera operator (if no camera is
available, use some other object and pretend it is a camera), and
maybe even a trenchcoat and hat to help set the stage.

LEADER: Good morning, good to see you all! Do you ever watch
the news on TV? Sometimes they interview people on the news,
and this morning I'd like to interview you. Let's pretend that I'm
a reporter and that you are just coming out of church on a Sunday
morning. Let's pretend that the steps here are the steps that lead
out of the church. So what you all need to do is to line up like
you're leaving the church and in just a minute we'll come out of
the church and be interviewed. Now don't all come at once, just
a few at a time.

(*With camera pointed toward you and the children behind you,
use your best TV reporter voice.*) Good morning ladies and gen-
tlemen, Brant Baker, WPPC News (*use your own name and*

church initials), here reporting on something strange. For the last several weeks people have been seen coming out of the building you can see behind me. Speculation has run high as to what it is they do there. We're here to ask them. (*Nod to first children.*) Here come some of them now. Excuse me, ma'am, could you tell us what it is you have been doing in there?
CHILD: Well, we're worshiping God.
L: Worshiping God. Thank you. Yes sir, could I ask you next, tell us what it is you like best about worshiping God.
CHILD: Talking to God.
L: You like talking to God best, I see. Thank you. Yes sir, please tell us what it is you like the best about worshiping God?
C: Um . . . I like . . . I don't know.
L: Well said! Thank you sir! Is there someone else to interview? Please come forward, yes sir, and you too ma'am, one last question. Tell me, why do you do it? What makes you want to do it?
C: Because Jesus loves us.
L: I see, that is a good reason. Well, thank you. This is Brant Baker, WPPC News, signing off.

You all did very well! We got some interesting insights! Let's have a prayer and thank God that we have a place we can worship. (*Prayer.*)

ACTION!

Scripture: Psalm 95:1-7
Focus: Perhaps it is our culture, perhaps the configuration of most sanctuaries, but somehow the notion persists of worship as entertainment. One small clue is when people refer to the congregation as the "audience." In fact, this perception is just opposite of what it should be: worship is participation, not entertainment.
Experience: To come before God as the actors rather than the audience.
Arrangements: None are needed.

LEADER: Good morning. How many of you have ever seen a play? Most of you have. Well then, you know that when there is a play, like at school, all of the audience sits in seats down on the floor, so let's all move down to the floor (*for instance, off the chancel steps onto the sanctuary floor*) and become an audience. Now the actors and actresses stand up on the stage (*stand up on the chancel and ad lib with as much ham as can be mustered*) and say something like "To be, or not to be, that is the question. Whether 'tis nobler . . ." you know how that goes.

But what would happen if you went to see a play and they said, "Oh, you're the audience—good. Will the audience please come up on stage?" And you all had to move up here (*motion children to move to chancel area*). "Everybody up on the stage, that's where the audience is going to stand."

And then the actors said, "We're going to sit down here" (*take a seat in one of the first pews*) and then they said, "OK, go ahead." What would you do? (*Fall silent for at least five to ten seconds.*)

CHILDREN: (*Silence.*)

L: Well, that's kind of a problem, isn't it? But you know, that's exactly what we do every Sunday. We come to perform a service for God, to worship God, and what do we do? We sit down here, and we say, "OK, God, go ahead," and we think of God as up there on the stage instead of God being the audience, which is what God really is in our worship. What do you think we should do about that? If we're here to perform for God, what are some of the things that we can do for God when we're here?

C: Pray. Sing. Praise God. Do a responsive reading. Say "hi" to people.

L: Good answers! All of those things are part of our worship, the service that we perform for God without expecting God to perform for us. Let's have a prayer and ask God to help us worship. (*Prayer.*)

THE BODY
OF CHRIST

THE BODY OF CHRIST

Scripture: Romans 12:4-5; 1 Corinthians 12:14-26; Ephesians 4:15-16

Focus: The body of Christ is Paul's powerful image to describe the interrelated structure of the church. Each part needs the other, each part has a specific task that it is uniquely able to perform. The focus of this sermon is to explore what these different parts of the body are in a particular church.

Experience: To relate the parts of the body mentioned by Paul to specific groups within the church, by asking members of those groups to stand when they hear their group, and the corresponding part in the body you have assigned to it, called. Children will be asked to stand when they see their parents stand to form bridges from parent to child through church service groups.

Arrangements: You will need a list of the various parts of the body mentioned by Paul in 1 Corinthians, alongside a list of all the groups in your church.

LEADER: Good to see you today! I want to read to you a few verses from the Bible, from the book of Romans. "For as in one body we have many members, and not all the members have the same function, so we, who are many, are one body in Christ, and individually we are members one of another." A man named Paul wrote these words, and he is saying that a church is a lot like our body. Part of the church is a foot, part of it is a hand, part of it is an eye. Do you know which parts of our church are these things?

CHILDREN: No.

L: I thought you might not, so I made a list! (*To the congregation*) And how about standing when I call out a part of our church body that you're a member of. (*To children*) And how about standing when you see your parents stand, OK? Then here we go.

Foot	Mission Committee
Hand	Deacons
Ear	Naomi Women's Circle
Eye	Worship Committee
Arm	Hope Sunday School Class
Elbow	Christian Education Committee

(*Your list can be as brief or as comprehensive as you like. A good ending would be to ask everyone else to stand, too.*)

And now, will *all* of the other parts of this body of Christ please stand? (*To the children*) There's one very important part of the body that I didn't mention, the head. Who do you suppose is the head of the church?

c: The minister? My daddy? Jesus?

L: Some intriguing answers, but I think I'd have to agree that Jesus is the head of the church! Jesus is the one who tells all of the other parts what to do and then helps them do what they need to do.

Let's have a prayer, and since we're all standing up, let's all hold hands while we thank God that we are joined together in one body, with Jesus Christ as our head. (*Prayer.*)

CONNECTIONS

Scripture: 1 John 3:11
Season/Sunday: Homecoming
Focus: One of the things it means to be the body of Christ is that we share a unity with all Christians everywhere. The focus of this sermon is to affirm the unity and oneness of the church universal.
Experience: To be joined together, hand in hand, so that the entire church is connected. The children will assume positions at the end of each pew, or row of chairs, so that they start the joining of hands and bridge across the aisles.
Arrangements: None are needed.

LEADER: Will the children please meet me in the middle of the church? Good morning! Does anybody know what special day today is in the life of our church?

CHILDREN: Homecoming.

L: Homecoming, that's right. And that means we've had a lot of people come from all sorts of places, from all over, to be home with us here today. One of the reasons that they can come back and say that this is their home is because we believe that in Jesus Christ we are all part of one church; in love we're all in touch with other Christians all over the world. To understand this a little better it might be fun if we played a game today, a game to put us in touch with everybody. What we all need to do is stand at the end of a row, everybody go stand at the end of any pew, maybe pretend that you're someplace far away, and hold the hand of the first person sitting in the pew. Then that person should hold the hand of the person who is next to him or her, so that we'll all be connected. Is everybody holding somebody's hand? Now, all the children should join hands across the aisle to make one long chain. Are you folks up in the balcony holding hands? Choir, are you playing? Good.

One of the reasons we can come home is because we are part of a much larger church, the church of Jesus Christ, and we're connected with Christians around the whole world. Let's have a prayer and thank God for giving us this special fellowship. (*Prayer.*)

WHAT'S YOUR LABEL?

Scripture: Galatians 3:26
Focus: Knowing who or what we belong to is an important way in which we build our identity as people. As Christians we belong unshakably to God. The focus of this sermon is to establish that identity and belonging.
Experience: To discuss putting labels on things as a way we show to whom they belong, and then to have a special label put on the children showing to whom they belong.
Arrangements: You will need labels (the standard nametag used in many churches would do nicely) that read "This Child of God Belongs to Jesus" in sufficient number for each child to have one. Give these to some likely person in the congregation (a Sunday school teacher known by most of the children, another minister, a prominent leader in the church) who can supply them on cue.

LEADER: Hello! How are you today? I have a question for you. Have you ever put your name on something to show that it's yours?
CHILDREN: Yes. No, but my Mommy did.
L: What kind of things do you put your name on?
C: Jacket. Book. Lunch box.
L: Good answers! Well, what about you, who do you belong to?
C: Nobody. Mommy and Daddy. Myself.

L: I heard a lot of answers, and there seems to be some confusion. Does anybody have a label to show who they belong to?
C: No!
L: Hmmm. I wonder if the Bible might help us here. It says in the book of Galatians, ". . . in Christ Jesus you are all children of God, through faith." If we are all children of God, that would seem to mean that we really belong to God. But there's still no label. (*Cue.*)
MEMBER: I have some labels that might work.
L: You do? Let's see . . . (*read label*), "This Child of God belongs to Jesus." These are perfect, thanks! (*Begin putting labels on children, front or back.*) Now we can know for sure who we belong to, just like it says in the Bible. We are all children of God, and we all belong to Jesus because we believe. This is wonderful!

Let's have a prayer and thank God that we belong to Jesus. (*Prayer.*)

GOSPEL HUGS

Scripture: 1 Corinthians 12; Romans 16:16
Season/Sunday: Evangelism or Guest Sunday
Focus: As parts of the body of Christ, each of us, child or adult, has a unique and important role in the life of the church, including its outreach and fellowship. Sometimes our "gift in the body" can be as simple as a hug.
Experience: To share the message of the love of Jesus Christ through a hug.
Arrangements: None are needed, but do decide ahead of time whether you will ask the children to hug anybody (preferably somebody they don't know) or only people visiting the church that morning.

LEADER: Good to see you all, how are you all doing today? You know, one of the very special talents that you all have is the way you can help people feel loved by sharing your own love with them. What are some of the ways we show people we love them?
CHILDREN: Be nice.

L: Anything else? Is there a way you have in your family to physically show your love? (*Hug yourself to give the hint.*)
c: Hug. Kiss.
L: A hug! A hug is a wonderful thing, isn't it? Hey, I've got an idea . . . what if we were to go out and give hugs to some of the congregation, you know, as a way of telling them that God loves them and that we love them?
c: (*Nod agreement.*)
L: Well, let's do it! (*You may need to stand up to get them started.*) Try and find somebody you don't know and give them a big hug! (*Children should go out into the congregation and start giving hugs.*)

(*As children reassemble*) You know, sometimes we as children may think that we don't have a lot to offer to adults in church. But a hug is one of the most wonderful things in the world that you can give somebody, because it helps to make folks comfortable. Giving a hug is a wonderful gift that you have to give, an important gift, one of your gifts that you have in the church. Let's hold hands and thank God for how we can use our gift to spread God's love. (*Prayer.*)

CHURCH HUG

Scripture: 1 John 4:7
Focus: In an increasingly unsafe and suspicious world, the church is one of the few places outside the home where we know we are safe and loved. The focus of this sermon is to demonstrate and celebrate this freedom to love in the church, because we are "of God."
Experience: To form a love huddle, essentially a giant group hug.
Arrangements: None are needed.

LEADER: Good morning. You know, in the church, in Jesus Christ, we have a special kind of friendship with one another, a friendship that isn't like any other friendship we have anywhere else. It's a friendship that helps us love everyone in the church, even if we don't know them all that well. How can we do that? What makes it possible for us to love all the other people in the church?

CHILDREN: Love. God.

L: That's right! It's love, God's love, love that God has given to us that we then give to everyone else. Well, what do you do when you love somebody?

c: Pray for them. Give them presents. Be nice to them.

L: Anything else? When you want to show your mom or dad you love them what do you do?

c: Clean up your room. Kiss them. Hug them.

L: Good! Well, of all those things—prayer, presents, clean rooms, hugs and kisses—maybe we can use one to show each other our love right now. What if we were to have one big giant hug? Let's all stand up, and (*to two of the children*) would you two hug each other? Great. Now all of you (*indicating the children immediately around them*) hug them . . . and all of us get in here and hug. (*Lots of giggling; join hug on your knees.*) Isn't this great?

c: YES!

L: While we're still hugging, let's have a prayer and thank God for the special love we have for each other in the church because of Jesus Christ. (*Prayer.*)

HUG COUPONS

Scripture: Ecclesiastes 3:1, 5

Focus: In an increasingly unsafe and suspicious world, the church is one of the few places outside the home where we know we are safe and loved. The focus of this sermon is to demonstrate and celebrate this freedom to love in the church.

Experience: To exchange a "Hug Coupon" for a hug with each child, and then send them into the congregation to exchange their coupons for hugs from people there. The congregation should continue exchanging the coupons with one another and with the children (the idea is *not* to hold on to the coupon) until you finally have to stop the uproar!

Arrangements: You will need to make copies of the "Hug Coupon" printed below (or better yet, design your own) in sufficient number that each child will actually take two or three out into the congregation, plus enough for you to keep some so that if children return early you can re-hug them and send them out with another coupon.

LEADER: It's really wonderful to see all of you today! And may I say that you are all looking especially huggable today, too! Did you know that people in the Bible hugged?
CHILDREN: Yes. No.
L: There was a lot of hugging, but the clearest place is in a book called Ecclesiastes, where it says, "For everything there is a season, and a time for every matter under heaven, a time to [hug], and a time to refrain from [hugging]." This morning it's time to hug! I've got some Hug Coupons that I'm going to give each one of you in exchange for a hug. (*Begin distributing and hugging while you talk.*) After you get a Hug Coupon you need to go out

into the congregation and find someone, give that person the coupon, and get a hug back. Here, take a couple. (*To congregation, while you continue hugging and distributing*) Congregation, the idea here is for you to get rid of that coupon, which means you're going to have to exchange it with someone else for a hug.

(As children return, send them back out with more coupons, perhaps directing them to unhugged people or areas in the congregation. Go out and do some hugging yourself with your extra coupons!)

OK! It's time to refrain from hugging! Will the children come on back, please? Let's have a prayer and thank God for the fun and the love we can share when we hug, and after church today you can exchange a few more coupons if you want to. *(Prayer.)*

FALL ON YOUR FACE!

Scripture: 2 Samuel 7:18; Luke 22:41; Matthew 26:39 (RSV); Mark 11:25

Focus: Singing, the sacraments, and this collection of children's sermons all suggest that our bodies, as well as our minds, are involved in worship. The focus of this sermon is to explore the biblical use of our body in prayer.

Experience: To assume different positions for prayer found in the Bible.

Arrangements: You will need a Bible with passages marked.

LEADER: Good morning, good to see you, good to see everybody! I have a question for you today. What do we do when we pray? How do we get ready to pray?

CHILDREN: Put our hands together.

L: Right. What else?

C: Bow our heads.

L: Bow our heads, good, what else?

C: Close our eyes.

L: Right, close our eyes. And we always do that, right? No matter what the rest of our body is doing, we can do those three things. Well, did you ever think about the position that your body is in when you pray? I'd like to read to you from the Bible some positions for praying. And as I read these different positions would you be willing to do them? The first one is from 2 Samuel and this is the only place, the only place in the whole Bible, that talks about sitting as a position when we pray to God. It says, "Then

King David went in and *sat* before the Lord, and said, 'Who am I, O Lord God, and what is my house, that you have brought me thus far?' " Is everybody sitting?

The next one is from Luke and it's about Jesus. "Then [Jesus] withdrew from them about a stone's throw, *knelt* down, and prayed . . ." So everybody kneel. Everybody on their knees . . .

c: (*General movement and giggling.*)

L: Good! That's kneeling. Here's another one. This one's also about Jesus and it's from Matthew. "And going a little farther he *fell on his face* and prayed." Oh boy! Everybody fall on your face!

c: (*Much giggling.*)

L: OK, stay there! This is the last one and it's from Mark, "Whenever you *stand* praying . . ." Whenever you stand, everybody stand . . .

c: Ohhhh. (*Much disappointment in having to get up.*)

L: Let's stay standing and have our own prayer thanking God we can worship even by the way our bodies are when we pray. (*Prayer.*)

VOICES

Scripture: Psalm 117
Focus: Singing, the sacraments, and this collection of children's sermons all suggest that our bodies, as well as our minds, are involved in worship. The focus of this sermon is to explore the biblical use of our voice in worship.
Experience: To offer vigorous verbal praise (shout) while learning a "new" word ("Hallelujah").
Arrangements: None are needed.

LEADER: Good morning. Smile! How's everybody? Everybody gather in close. I'd like to teach you a little bit of a foreign language today called Hebrew. Hebrew is what they spoke a long time ago, in the time of the Old Testament. The first word I want to teach you is the name of God. God's name, in Hebrew, is Yahweh. Can you all say "Yahweh?"

CHILDREN: Yahweh.

L: Very good! That's God's name, but in Old Testament times people didn't say that name because it was very, very holy. So, many times what they would say was simply "Ya."

C: Ya.

L: Ya! Sounds like you're agreeing with somebody, doesn't it?! OK, the next word I'd like to teach you is "hallel," can you say "hallel?"

C: Hallel.

L: Good! *Hallel* is a word that means "to praise." And if you put a "u" on the end of it, it becomes a command, "hallelu." Can you say "hallelu?"

C: Hallelu.

L: All right! So, if you wanted to say "Praise God" what would you say?

C: (*Silence.*)

L: (*Prompting*) How would you say "Praise God?"

C: Praise God?

L: Praise God . . . uh, well, that would be one way to do it! You got me on that one! What if you wanted to say it in Hebrew? Could you say "hallelu" and then say "ya?" Let's all say it together . . .

C: Hallelu . . . ya.

L: I bet whenever you heard the choir, or anybody, say "Hallelujah" you probably thought, "Oh, that's just some English word I don't understand." But it's really Hebrew, and it means "Praise the Lord!" It's a command. Praise the Lord!

OK, let's try something else. Let's all say "Hallelujah" real softly, just mumble it.

C: (softly) Hallelujah . . .

L: Do you feel very praise-ful? Does that really speak to your heart? No. What if you said (*yelling*) "Hallelujah!" Try that, on three, everybody ready? One, two, three . . .

C: Hallelujah!

L: Now do you feel like you are praising? Does that help you feel a little more excited about praise? Let's see if we can teach the congregation. Congregation, let's hear you praise God by saying "Hallelujah." Ready? One, two, three . . .

C: Hallelujah.

L: How do you feel? I'm going to ask the congregation to try that and to yell it out, but you know they're grown-ups, so they're going to need your help. On three, one, two, three . . .

EVERYBODY: Hallelujah!

L: (*To children*) What do you think, can they do better than that? Once more on three. One, two, three . . .

EVERYBODY: Hallelujah!

L: Very good! You see, we human beings are kind of funny. What we do with our voices can speak to our hearts. So if we say (*mumbling*) "Hallelujah" we probably won't feel very praise-ful, our spirit doesn't get excited. But if we say (*loudly*) "Hallelujah!" then our spirit says, "Yes! Hallelujah!"

Let's have a prayer and praise God. (*Prayer.*)

HANDS

Scripture: Psalm 134:2; Hebrews 4:14; Matthew 8:2-3; Luke 6:38; Psalm 47:1

Focus: Singing, the sacraments, and this collection of children's sermons all suggest that our bodies, as well as our minds, are involved in worship. The focus of this sermon is to explore the biblical use of part of our body.

Experience: To explore biblical suggestions of the use we make of our hands in worship.

Arrangements: You will need a Bible with passages marked.

LEADER: Good morning. I have a question for you this morning. What is this? (*Hold up your hand.*)

CHILDREN: Five. Hand.

L: A five, right, and a hand, right. Why did God create hands? What are they for?

C: Picking up. Touch. To use. To work with.

L: Good answers. You know, the Bible talks about our hands. Why don't we look for a few minutes at some of the things the Bible says we can do with our hands. Let's stand up . . . and let's say that whatever we hear read in the Bible we're going to do, OK?

In Psalm 134 it says, "Lift up your hands to the holy place, and bless the Lord." So we can lift up our hands and worship. Keep 'em up!

Another thing it says here in Hebrews is "let us hold fast to our confession," and holding is something we do with our hands. How do we hold fast our confession, what does that mean? Well, we might hug ourselves, hug our hearts, like we were saying that we're going to hold on tight to what we believe.

In Matthew it says "and there was a leper who came to [Jesus] and knelt before him, saying, 'Lord if you choose, you can make me clean.' He stretched out his hand and touched him, saying, 'I do choose. Be made clean!' " So hands can be used also for healing . . . maybe we could all touch somebody, gently and in love, and keep on touching them for a minute . . .

In Luke it says something a little different we can do with our hands, it says, "Give, and it will be given to you. A good measure, pressed down, shaken together, running over, will be put into your lap; for the measure you give will be the measure you get back." So hands can be used for giving. How can we give to others with our hands? What do we have to give with our hands? Well, we could hug somebody else. Let's all turn to the person next to us and give them a hug. Give them a big ol' hug.

A passage from the Psalms says, "Clap your hands, all you peoples . . ." (*Children begin clapping*) Right, clap! The Bible seems to be saying that clapping our hands is something we can do with our hands, and that it pleases God. I bet you didn't know there were so many things you could do in church with your hands! Well, let's all hold hands and have a prayer thanking God for making us so wondrously. (*Prayer.*)

LEGS

Scripture: Psalm 135:1-2
Focus: Singing, the sacraments, and this collection of children's sermons all suggest that our bodies, as well as our minds, are involved in worship. The focus of this sermon is to explore the biblical use of part of our body.

Experience: To explore a biblical suggestion of the use we can make of our legs in worship.
Arrangements: None are needed

LEADER: Good morning . . . I'd like to read to you from Psalm 135:1-2 "Praise the Lord! Praise the name of the Lord; give praise, O servants of the Lord, you that *stand* in the house of the Lord." Why do we stand up in worship? Do we do it just so we can stretch?
CHILDREN: No!
L: Well then, why do we stand up during worship?
C: To show God we love him.
L: I think that's right. In a way, every time we stand up in church— whether we stand up to sing a hymn, or if we stand up to pray, or if we stand up to say the Affirmation of Faith—every time we stand up, we're saying "I love you, God." Let's try that, let's stand up, and as we stand let's say "I love you, God."
C: (*Children stand*) I love you, God.
L: (*After sitting*) Should we do it again?
C: (*Standing again*) I love you, God!
L: (*After sitting*) That was pretty good. Let's try it one more time!
C: (*Standing again, louder*) I love you, God!
L: Amen! Let's hold hands and have a prayer to thank God for giving us bodies that we can use to glorify and worship and love God. (*Prayer.*)

KNEES

Scripture: Psalm 95:6-7, Ephesians 3:14-19
Focus: Singing, the sacraments, and this collection of children's sermons all suggest that our bodies, as well as our minds, are involved in worship. The focus of this sermon is to explore the biblical use of part of our body.
Experience: To explore biblical suggestions of the use we make of our knees in worship.
Arrangements: You will need a Bible with passages marked.

LEADER: Come on over here, we've got plenty of room for everyone! Good to see you all this morning, how is everybody? I want to talk with you about something that is very important . . . knees! How many knees have you got?

CHILDREN: Two! Three . . .

L: Three! Good for you, you're way ahead of the rest of us. All right, we've all got knees . . . what are knees for?

C: Bending. Walking. Doing exercise.

L: Good answers. Well, what about in the church, do we use our knees in the church?

C: To sit?

L: To sit, good. Have you ever seen anybody kneel in a church sometimes?

C: Kneel to take communion.

L: Good. And sometimes to pray, and sometimes when we ordain people we see them kneel. Why do you suppose that we kneel in the church for some of these things? Why not standing or sitting or standing on our heads? (*Silence.*) Well I'll tell you a secret . . . the word in Hebrew that means "knees" is *barach*. Can you say that?

C: Barach!

L: And the word that means "blessing" in Hebrew is . . . can you guess what it is? It's *barach!* It's the same word! So there seems to be something about being on our knees and about being blessed. So I think we better get on our knees right now—everybody on our knees. (*Move to kneeling position.*) There's something about being on our knees that puts us in a right position to be blessed by God, somehow maybe we feel closer to God when we're on our knees.

C: We're littler too!

L: I guess that's right! Let's hold hands and have a prayer and thank God for knees. (*Prayer.*)

FEET

Scripture: 1 Chronicles 28:2; Psalm 91:13; Psalm 119:101; Matthew 10:14; Joshua 5:15 (RSV)

Focus: Singing, the sacraments, and this collection of children's sermons all suggest that our bodies, as well as our minds, are

involved in worship. The focus of this sermon is to explore the
biblical use of part of our body.

Experience: To explore biblical suggestions of the use we make of
our feet in service and worship.

Arrangements: You will need a Bible with passages marked.

LEADER: Good morning! Hope everyone is doing great today!
Let me ask you a question. What are feet for?

CHILDREN: Walking. Standing. Jumping.

L: Good answers! Did you know that people in the Bible had
feet, too? And that sometimes they used their feet to help them
do things for God? Why don't we look at some places in the
Bible that mention people's feet, and then we'll try and do what
it says those people did, OK?

C: OK!

L: Here's a verse in 1 Chronicles that says, "King David rose to
his feet." Well, somebody said feet were used for standing, it
must have been that way in the Old Testament too! Let's stand
up! (*All stand.*)

A verse in Psalm 91 says, "the serpent you will trample under
foot." Hmmm. Trample, that's like stomping, I guess. Let's pretend we're stomping on a serpent!

C: (*Laughter as they stomp their feet.*)

L: OK! The next verse is Psalm 119:101. It says, "I hold back
my feet from every evil way, in order to keep your word." That's
important, isn't it? To hold our feet so that we don't walk into
bad places. Well, let's hold our feet! (*Bend over and grab your
feet.*)

C: (*Should do the same.*)

L: They evidently had feet in the New Testament too, because in
Matthew Jesus told his disciples, "If any one will not welcome
you or listen to your words, shake off the dust from your feet."
Shake your feet!

C: I'm shaking off the dust!

L: You sure are! Great, well, stop shaking for a minute because
we have one more thing for our feet to do. In Joshua 5:15 an
angel tells Joshua, "Put off your shoes from your feet; for the
place where you stand is holy." Wow, do you think the place
where we are standing now could be holy too?

C: Yes. No.

L: I guess it wouldn't hurt to be on the safe side if it was. After all, this is God's house. Let's all take off our shoes! (*Take off your shoes.*)

C: (*Giggle as they take shoes off.*)

L: (*Holding shoes*) Let's have a prayer and thank God for our feet and for being able to stand on holy ground and worship God. (*Prayer.*)

SACRAMENTS

REMEMBERING OUR BAPTISM

Scripture: Acts 2:38-39; Exodus 12:26-27
Season/Sunday: Baptism or Dedication
Focus: In most traditions, members of the congregation participate in the baptism or dedication of a baby by making promises to help the parents in providing a Christian education. The focus of this sermon is the continuation of those promises by the congregation.
Experience: To have the congregation repeat the promise made at the baptism or dedication of a baby, having each child supply his or her own name at the appropriate place in the service.
Arrangements: A copy of denominational service of baptism or dedication will be needed.

LEADER: Good morning. Good to see everybody today! How many of you remember when you were baptized? Raise your hand if you remember . . . only one or two. Well, you might not remember but on the day that you were baptized, all these people stood up and promised to take care of you, to teach you the gospel of Jesus Christ, and to be here when you needed help. Since most of us don't remember, how about if we did at least part of what happened that day again? What I would like you to do is to say your name into the microphone when I give it to you, OK? Would the congregation please stand.

"Our Lord Jesus Christ ordered us to teach those who are baptized. Do you, the people of the church, promise to tell . . . *(ask children to say their names)*

CHILDREN: Jamie, Andrea, Baron, Brandon, Christie, Carolyn, Lisa, Missy, Darren, Allison, Mark, Josh.

L: . . . the Good News of the gospel, do you promise to help them know all that Christ commands, and by your fellowship and love do you promise to strengthen their family ties with the household of God?" Do you?

CONGREGATION: We do.

L: Amen. Let's pray and thank God for all these people who have promised to tell us the gospel, to take care of us in Jesus Christ, and to love us. *(Prayer.)*

A CHURCH FULL OF PARENTS

Scripture: Philippians 2:4
Season/Sunday: Baptism or Dedication
Focus: In the household of God, all Christian adults assume the role of parents (even those without children). This ministry of parenthood is a key part of the congregation's participation in a baptism or dedication.
Experience: To see all the "parents" a child of God has in the church. At a point in the sermon, while you talk about the focus, you will take children by the hand to stand with adults they may not know.
Arrangements: None are needed.

L: Would the children come forward at this time please? How are you doing? I've got a question for you, we'll see how you do on it. How many parents do you have?
CHILDREN: Two. One. Four. Two.
L: Everybody has at least one, right? OK, what do parents do for you?
C: Buy toys! Give us food and clothes. Care for us. They clean up. They help you. They love you. They take care of you. They fix breakfast.
L: Fix breakfast, that always was one of my favorites! So what I hear you saying is that our parents provide for us things like money and clothes and a warm house and breakfast, all that stuff. They correct us. If we do wrong they tell us so we don't get hurt; they maybe even punish us if we need that. And they provide a good example for us, right?

All right! Everybody in the congregation who does not have a child sitting down here, please stand up.

Do you know that you actually have more parents than you thought? Every one of these people who is standing up (*stand up and take two children by the hand and take them to someone who is standing*)—you come with me, and you come with me—is a parent, because when you were baptized or dedicated in this church or in another church all of these people agreed—here, these are your new parents—that they would provide money to help the church so that you could be educated—this is your new parent. (*Go back for two more children.*) All these people also agreed that they would teach you, and even discipline you, so that if you did something wrong, so that if you were swinging on the curtains in the fellowship hall, they would say 'Don't do that!'. . . . Here you go, this is your new parent, instant fatherhood, how about that? . . . They agreed they would be a model for you (*go back for two more children*), they would show you in worship what was right and what you needed to do, they would provide good examples for you in the community—here are your new parents—they would teach you by their example what was right . . . here's your new dad. All these people are your parents in Jesus Christ. So you don't have just one parent, or two parents, or even four parents, but you have an entire church full of parents.

Let's have a prayer, and let's thank God for all these parents. (*Prayer.*)

A GIFT FOR CAMIE

Scripture: Ephesians 4:11-13
Season/Sunday: Baptism or Dedication
Focus: On the occasion of a baptism or dedication not only adults are involved in the congregational promises. The children who come forward for the children's sermon may not be old enough now to care for the Christian education of the baby, but each child can still offer his or her own gift.
Experience: To have each child draw a picture or write a note as a gift for a newly baptized or dedicated baby, welcoming him or her to the church and fulfilling the congregation's promise to contribute to the child's knowledge of Jesus Christ.
Arrangements: To help the children in creating their picture gifts, you may want to pass out paper and crayons. Also, be sure some system is announced for collecting the finished products (during the time of the normal offering would have some nice overtones) and for passing the art on to the family to give to their child in years ahead.

LEADER: How's everybody? Good to see you all! A few minutes ago when we baptized Camie we all stood up. Did everybody do that?
CHILDREN: (*Most nod heads.*)
L: Why did we do that, why did we stand up, does anybody know? Do you remember that I said some words and asked the

congregation if they promised to teach Camie the gospel and all that Christ commands, and they all said "We do." Did you all say "We do?"

c: (*Most nod heads.*)

l: OK, now how are you going to do that? What are you going to teach her? Didn't know we really meant it, did you? Well, let me see if I can help. I brought some paper and some crayons, and what I thought we might do is take a few minutes during the service today and draw a picture that tells Camie God loves her or write something to Camie about how much God loves us or about something that Christ commands. Then at the time of the offering, later in the service, put them in the offering plate and we'll give them to Camie as our special gift to her. (*Distribute paper and crayons.*)

Let's have a prayer and thank God that we have something to give Camie and thank God that she is part of our church. (*Prayer.*)

SENSING THE WORD OF GOD

Scripture: Matthew 26:26-27
Season/Sunday: Lord's Supper
Focus: The Word of God comes to us in many forms. The Lord's Supper is one of those forms, but is unique in its communication to us through our physical selves.
Experience: To become aware that we receive God's Word in various ways, and to experience that Word with the full variety of our senses.
Arrangements: You will need a Bible and a picture or other visual representation of the bread (wheat) and wine (grapes), perhaps as part of a stained-glass window or wood carving on the front of the communion table. Presumably this sermon will be used on a day when communion is being celebrated, so the communion table will be spread.

LEADER: Hello everybody, good to see you today. I'd like to read to you something Jesus said: "Take, eat, this is my body . . . Drink from it all of you; for this is my blood of the covenant . . ." What did we do just now?

CHILDREN: (*A certain guilty silence.*) Read the Bible?

L: Well, I read the Bible, what did you do?

C: Listened?

L: Listened, that's right! You heard the Word of God. OK, let's go over there. (*Move to visual representation of elements.*) Look up there. What's that a picture of?

C: A cup. Some grapes. Wheat.

L: Right, and what are we doing right now? (*Point at your eyes.*)

C: Looking?

L: Right! We're seeing the symbols for communion. Great! OK, everybody come with me up to the front. So far we've heard and we've seen . . . what's this? (*Point to Lord's Supper.*)

C: Food!

L: Food, and we call this food the Lord's Supper. Later on in the service what are we going to do?

C: Eat?

L: We're going to eat! God has given us so many ways to learn about God's Word! We can hear the Word of God, we can see the Word of God, and we can eat, or taste, the Word of God. And all these things are ways God has to remind us that God's Word to us is that we are loved by God.

Let's have a prayer and thank God for giving us all these ways to know of God's Word and of God's love. (*Prayer.*)

CELEBRATING COMMUNION AROUND THE WORLD

Scripture: Galatians 3:26-28
Season/Sunday: World Communion Sunday
Focus: One of the things we affirm as Christians is that all of the various churches, when taken together, are the one body of Jesus Christ. On World Communion Sunday we celebrate that oneness by knowing that Christians around the world are sharing the Lord's Supper on this same day, transcending geographical and even political barriers.
Experience: To become the globe, with representatives from cities around the world.
Arrangements: There are at least two ways this sermon could be done. The first is as presented below, with the children circling around the table and representing the global community as they pass the cup and say the brief prayer. For this version you will need a list of cities in different time zones. Another option would be to visit an adult Sunday school class before church and hand out eighteen copies of the list of cities, assigning one per person. Their instructions would be to stand up, after a signal from you, wherever they are in the sanctuary and read the names of their assigned city in the order it appears. The children could respond as a group with the brief prayer after each city has been called out. In this case the "globe" would be represented by people standing up all over the congregation.

LEADER: Good morning! Let's make a big circle around the communion table, and let's make it big enough so there is room for everybody, so that we're all in a circle around the table. Today is World Communion Sunday, which is a very special day because it means that all over the world, all around the world (*motion to circle as if it were the world*) Christians are celebrating communion. What if we did something to remind ourselves that every hour during this day somewhere, somebody is celebrating the Lord's Supper? How about if I give someone the cup, and then read the name of a city somewhere in the world saying "In such-and-such a city . . . ," and then have the person holding the cup say ". . . we thank God for sending Jesus Christ." In a way, each one of us will become a representative of the Christians in that city. Will you take the cup? . . . thanks. OK, here we go: In Mexico City, Mexico . . .

CHILD: . . . we thank God for sending Jesus Christ.

L: Good! Would you like to hold it next? I need some volunteers! Thank you. In Los Angeles, U.S.A. . . .

CHILD: . . . we thank God for sending Jesus Christ. (*Repeat this process using these or other cities.*)

L: Vancouver, Canada
      Papeete, Tahiti
      Honolulu, U.S.A.
      Pago Pago, Samoa
      Christchurch, New Zealand
      Sidney, Australia
      Tokyo, Japan
      Seoul, Korea
      Saigon, Vietnam
      Bangkok, Thailand
      Kabul, Afghanistan
      Tehran, Iran
      Moscow, U.S.S.R
      Rome, Italy
      London, England
      your hometown

Great! You did a good job and reminded us that all around the world today Christians are celebrating God sending Jesus Christ. Let's all hold hands and have a prayer thanking God for giving us such a good way to remember that in communion, and for all the Christians all over the world today who are our brothers and sisters. (*Prayer.*)

AFTERWORD

The children's sermons offered in this book have grown from an understanding of a few basic developmental and educational insights, based on the work of Piaget, Erikson, Groome, and Wink. As described in the introduction, these children's sermons seek to *incarnate* the word of God.

From Jean Piaget we have gleaned information about the ways in which children think. This information led us away from children's sermons that are abstract and need reflection toward children's sermons that are experiential.

From Erik Erikson we saw that children in these age groups have certain tasks that emerge as part of their development. These tasks suggested that children's sermons should include movement (initiative), and a sense of working together to actually *make* the children's sermon (industry).

From Thomas Groome and from Walter Wink came the framework for educational methods that look for appropriation of a lesson and a subsequent "transformation" of a student. These methods gave rise to children's sermons that engage the imagination (as well as the body) to fix the message of the sermon firmly in a child's mind.

It is my hope that you have been able to see these insights applied in sermons you have utilized from this book and that you too are beginning to think in terms of experiential Christianity. There is a wealth of scripture to spark your imagination, a wealth of church geography to explore, and a wealth of God's own creativity within you waiting to be expressed. Go, thou, and do likewise!

But the insights of Piaget, Erikson, Groome, and Wink need not be limited to this one application. The ideas found in these pages can and should be employed in numerous settings. A Sunday school class could use one of these sermons as a discussion starter. In some cases an entire lesson could be built around the imagined world we create in the classroom, staying in character and "in place" for the entire class.

Or why not use some interactive experiences in a vacation Bible school? Often the curricula for these summer programs are built around the rich and colorful stories of biblical characters (Abraham, Moses or Joshua, David or Elijah, Jesus, Peter or Paul), stories that form the basis for many of the sermons in this book. An opening (or closing) convocation of all the classes in VBS acting out the crossing of the river Jordan or the feeding of the five thousand will probably make a more lasting impression than a flannel graph or filmstrip.

Experiential Christianity can be used with older youth as well. I once did a Bible study with a group of senior high youth on Jesus' stilling of the sea. We arranged our chairs in rows of three or four, as if they were bench seats across a small boat (the group could even outline the boat in masking tape on the floor). I stood at the "bow" with a Bible and told the story as we all swayed with the "waves" in ever-increasing pitch. (Be sure to start slow if you use this, so you have someplace to go!) When we finally woke Jesus and he calmed the waves and the wind, the stillness of soul was experienced even more deeply by a stillness of body.

Limiting these insights to work with children and youth would be as unthinkable as limiting their application to children's sermons. In many ways adults may be even better candidates for experiential learning because they have a broader base of experience from which to draw, and because they have the chance so infrequently. The main hurdle is to grant the freedom for using imagination. And sometimes that may mean being sneaky.

On one occasion the basic premise of a sermon found in this book was used with a woman's Bible study class, unbeknownst to them. When members of the group met on that particular Saturday morning, they found a note on the door saying that the meeting location had been changed and directing them to another room. When they arrived, a second note, saying basically the same thing, directed them to a third location. At the fifth location the faithful were welcomed with coffee and donuts, and a study of Elijah in 1 Kings 18:41-46 (see "Faithfulness" pages 28–29).

From this beginning came an increasing willingness to do more imaginative and experiential work. Later in the study we looked at Peter's prayer over the dead Tabitha in Acts 9. By that time we had no trouble finding women in the study to weep as the widows in Joppa wept, nor in finding a woman to lie "dead" on the table. And this with Presbyterians!

An all-church retreat is an ideal time to bring children, youth, and adults together for experiential encounters. Can you imagine a retreat on "The Body of Christ" with *everyone* (including the pastor) participating in some of the sermons described in that section of this book? And yet what a wonderful way for young and old to learn together and from one another what voices and hands and knees and feet are for!

The point is that experiential Christianity can be applied not only in worship but in virtually any educational setting in the church. Often these kinds of activities can be found in existing lessons, but as things to be done if there is extra time. Be encouraged to take any one of these children's sermons and use it as the basis of an educational *experience* in a classroom, on a retreat, or any place people have gathered to *experience* the truth and presence of God.

God bless.

NOTES

1. David Ng and Virginia Thomas, *Children in the Worshiping Community* (Atlanta: John Knox Press, 1981), 43.

2. Barbel Inhelder and Jean Piaget, *The Growth of Logical Thinking From Childhood to Adolescence,* trans. Anne Parsons and Stanley Milgram (New York: Basic Books, Inc., 1958).

3. Ibid., 35.

4. Erik Erikson, *Identity: Youth and Crisis* (New York: W.W. Norton & Company, 1968), 115–128.

5. Thomas H. Groome, *Christian Religious Education: Sharing Our Story and Vision* (San Francisco: Harper & Row, 1980), pp. 207–223.

6. Ibid., 207–208.

7. Walter Wink, *Transforming Bible Study* (Nashville: Abingdon,1980), 32.

3 9371 00009 0183

INDEX OF BIBLE PASSAGES

The number following each passage refers to the page of the children's sermon upon which it occurs.